Openings Into Ministry

Edited By
Ross Snyder

EXPLORATION PRESS

Chicago, Illinois 60637

This volume is one of the publications in the "Studies in Ministry and Parish Life" series published by the Exploration Press of The Chicago Theological Seminary.

253 W
Op2
81072320

Copyright © 1977 by Exploration Press of The Chicago Theological Seminary

Printed in the United States of America

All rights reserved. No part of this book may be reproduced or transmitted in any form or by any means, electronic or mechanical, including photo copying, recording, or any information storage and retrieval system, without permission in writing from the publisher.

Exploration Press
of
The Chicago Theological Seminary
5757 University Avenue
Chicago, Illinois 60637

ISBN: Cloth: 0-913552-10-0
       Paper: 0-913552-11-9

Library of Congress Catalog Card Number: 77-92707

Table of Contents

Section I Congregation-Pastor

IMAGES CONTAINING FUTURES	
Congregation Pastor	*Ross Snyder*
REVITALIZING A CONGREGATION	*John Tien*
HOW A CHURCH BEGAN	*Frazier Odom*
MINISTRY TO THE AGING	*Tom Evans*
ACTIVE, POTENT, DESIRABLE MINISTER	*Roy Larson and Ross Snyder*
A PROFESSIONAL TEAM	*Charles Burns*
IMAGE Sociality	*Ross Snyder*

Section II Membranes of Meaning

IMAGE Membranes of Meaning	*Ross Snyder*
A LIVED MOMENT REVISITED	*Franklin Elliott*
STORIFYING BY THE LISTENER	*Paul Davis*
A PASTORAL PERSPECTIVE ON FAMILY COUNSELING	*John Patton*
THE CRY OF THE HEART FOR HOME	*Truman Morrison*
I AM A SURGEON	*Mark Snyder M.D.*
IMAGE Conceptualized Primordial	*Ross Snyder*

Section III Celebrative Education

IMAGE Forming Form	*Ross Snyder*
THE INTENTIONAL SAPLING	*Richard Fisher*
FOR THE RELIGIOUS HUNGER OF INNER CITY CHILDREN	*David Henry*
BUILDING A CONGREGATION THROUGH INTERGENERATIONAL CELEBRATION	*Tom Chulak*
WONDER AS SACRAMENT	*Paul Wrightman*
A PROJECT IN FULLNESS OF LEARNING EUCHARIST	*Susan Bell*
IMAGE Appreciative Consummatory Consciousness	*Ross Snyder*

Section IV The Lord's Free People

IMAGES Psychohistory, Archetype, Christ the Transformer	*Ross Snyder*
THE CONSCIOUSNESS OF A PEOPLE	*Tom Cunningham*
A SOUTH AFRICAN BLACK CLASSROOM	*June Pym*
TOWARD SPIRITED EXISTENCE	*James Cochrane*
IMAGE Human Spirit	*Ross Snyder*

**Images
Containing Futures**

Section I
Congregation - Pastor

A CONGREGATION

1.
Persons
    Who believe in each other
        and in something together
Who are going thru heaven and hell
    and their transformations
        and have models of how to do it

2.
They meet regularly
    together thinking and feeling
        about the things that matter most
    once more re-meaning the events of their history
    voicing in public how it is with them
    singing, praying, yearning, treasuring, rejoicing
        until they are lifted into a Love and Truth
            which they are able to speak in language
                all human kind can understand

3.
Sometimes they experience the motion among them
    of the fellowship of Spirit thru the ages
Sometimes they are to God what the hand is to man

4.
A congregation is a message —
    "You are loved
        Help is available
            There is meeting where often persons are
            newborn again. Interwoven into a net where
            Spirit burns
We are in a great struggle
    The dark places of the earth are still full of

habitations of cruelty, but we are not overcome
We are learning the language of Spirit."

PASTOR

A pastor is one who has come thru religious experience
   has symbolized it as his own
      yet can speak of it in first-order language
         which moves his people
A pastor feels the mystery and extraordinary significance in the person before him
   helps him explore who he is before God
      and what he has to offer humankind
A pastor is
   a representative of something both are willing to serve
      connections with a Kingdom
         an ethically serious thinker
            a participant in regenerating the inner world or our time
               a developmental specialist
                  fighting for his people.

Revitalizing a Congregation and Pastor With the Help of the Erikson Developmental Story

JOHN W. TIEN
Bethany Reformed Church, Kalamazoo, Michigan

The personal problem to which this paper addresses itself is the lived moment of frustration that a pastor experiences when he feels that his effectiveness with a particular congregation no longer exists. Out of this frustration this pastor turned to some in depth introspection and to the developmental Epigenetic Life Cycle of Erikson for understanding and direction. This resulted in the use of the Erikson model in seeking to bring the congregation to an understanding of its own moment of existence and as a guide for building further ministry. It was assumed that a congregation has a group personality and a life development that can be looked at, and understood well enough by all that intervention can be made to bring new understanding and direction to the life of a specific group of people.

About three years ago I realized that I was continuing my ministry in a fit of frustration almost daily. The parish which I serve is one of many in the throes of having to adjust to urban change, which includes a changing neighborhood, a changing congregation, and a changing pastor with a changing family. My pastorate in this city began eleven years ago when nearly one third of the families of the church still lived in the immediate neighborhood. The leadership of the church was essentially the same as that of the past twenty years. However, many were close to the age of retirement. The average of the congregation of 790 was over 50 years of age. The membership included 70 widows and over 30 shut-ins. During the past eleven years over 70 of the active members have died. Many others have moved to retire in other areas. Most of the young people have attended college and very few have returned to this city. Many of the younger families who did remain have not felt a loyalty to the congregation and have joined churches in their neighborhoods or simply have become inactive.

The church today is largely made up of persons who are the descendents of the very early leadership of the church. Many of those who were responsible for the leadership of the church for the past twenty years have either retired or died. Some of these, who have remained, have been tremendously aware and helpful during this period of change. There are few families in the middle age years where one would normally look for leadership and organizational strength. There are very few young people in the 12-18 age group.

A concentrated effort was made to reach out to young couples about three years ago. As a result, we now have a growing number of younger couples in the church and a large number of children who are preschool and early elementary. The response of this new group gave me, as pastor, a new sense of hope. However, the continual need for readjustment was overwhelming. We felt the tension of continual urban change. We also felt the tension between the older elements of the congregation and the new young couples who were becoming part of the life of the church. In addition, there were conflicts within both groups because of differing values and a competing for leadership. My own personal life and my life with my family was beginning to be a real struggle as I immersed myself in seeking to develop understanding and communication in the life of a congregation which seemed to be growing apart.

Resistance to my leadership began to form with both overt and covert dimensions, and I began to feel a sense of powerlessness. The more I sought to throw myself into leadership formation the more resistance seemed to take place. Day followed day and week followed week with no meaning emerging. Looking back, I would describe those moments for all of us as walking into a darkened tunnel; the further we walked the darker it became.

Knowing I could not go on as things were, I was forced into a personal inventory, the likes of which I have never faced before. The real breakthrough was to admit that I was being dishonest with myself and with those around me. I was promising to deliver and driving myself harder and harder. Yet I was falling further and further behind and apart. My only sense of comfort was that many of my peers were experiencing similar kinds of struggles with their congregations in urban areas and feeling just as powerless. Programs that had produced support before now met with little or no results. "How-to" workshops and seminars, all the way from family growth to outreach and church growth, resulted in essentially no change. Each failure created more and more anxiety for me and the people of the congregation.

My honest searching led me to believe that our struggle lay in our lack of understanding in what was happening to ourselves in the growth and developmental process, in both personal and institutional dimensions. It was evident that change was having a dramatic effect upon all of our lives. Yet we were not understanding that change, much less were we able to manage the effect that change was having upon our lives. Many of us were losing our ability to remain human under the pressure of change. Through my own self-inventory my thoughts returned to Dr. Ross Snyder, under whom I had studied at Chicago Theological Seminary, and his concepts of phenomenalizing process, and the understanding of "lived moments." I was drawn again to the developmental task life story by Erik Erikson, particularly to those moments that Erikson describes as "Crises" in the growth and developmental process. (References are to **Identity: Youth and Crisis,** 1968.) I was struck with the possibility of using the Erikson model as a tool to describe and evaluate the growth and development of an institution such as the church, in this case the church of which I am pastor. Subsequently, I learned it could also be used as a tool by which to guide intervention.

APPLICATION OF THE MODEL

My first steps were largely those of conceptualization. I began to see the history of the church as a living process. The more I looked into old records and chatted with members who could remember the beginnings of the church and community, the more I saw parallels between personal growth and development (as conceived in Erikson's structure) and institutional growth and development. It seemed clear to me that the church had reached in its development the stage of GENERATIVITY vs. STAGNATION (Erikson, 1968, p. 94). If some new sense of hope was not forth coming the church would lose its sense of INTEGRITY and become a victim of DESPAIR. (Throughout this paper significant words taken from the Epigenetic Life-Cycle will be capitalized.)

It then became necessary to develop some form of communication whereby members of the congregation would be able to look at themselves objectively and collectively, both at their history and at their present moments of crisis. With the assistance of some very significant persons from the congregation we began to trace the history of the church with new meanings and hope. Together we developed a very non-professional slide series of the history of the church.

The slide series was divided into segments identified by the length of tenure of the pastors who gave leadership through the years. We included phases of building development to give a concreteness to the developmental concept. We began with the first little school house that was built in 1905 and included the building of two new churches, additions for larger seating capacity and rooms for Christian Education. We concluded with pictures of a complete refurnishing of the church building following a disastrous fire in 1972. It was at that time that the congregation had decided to remain in the inner city rather than to join in the flight to the suburbs. The basic content of the slides included pictures of persons, some of the founding fathers, the early church school classes, church organizations and pictures which depicted the many forms of ministry in which the church had been involved. These were prepared in such a way that they could be shown side by side with Erikson's "course of Life" model, projected through the use of an overhead projector.

It may be helpful to put the diagonal spiral of these eight developments of life before us in diagramatic form. The rest of the paper will make them come alive, so I hope.

TRUST	AUTONOMY	INITIATIVE	INDUSTRY
vs.	vs.	vs.	vs.
MISTRUST	SHAME, DOUBT	GUILT	INFERIORITY
IDENTITY	INTIMACY	GENERATIVITY	INTEGRITY
vs.	vs.	vs.	vs.
IDENTITY CONFUSION	ISOLATION	STAGNATION	DESPAIR

The basic purpose of preparing this presentation was for the members of the congregation to identify their own history, for them to see the changes which have taken place in the past, to recognize previous times of crises, and to be able to interpret that history as a process of development from which we need to plan for future development. Four basic questions were used through the process of viewing: (1) What have we experienced in the past? (2) What are we experiencing now? (3) Why are we experiencing what we feel? and (4) What steps do we need to take to rediscover a sense of resurrection within ourselves and to find the enabling power to move forward?

The initial presentation was given to the older adult class of the church which consists of about 50 members. This class represented much of the focus of resistance to myself as they fantasized about the years when "we had 600 in Sunday School." The fact that the original contract of four weeks was extended to six weeks attests to the positive reception given by the group. The presentation was heart warming. However, not without pain and stress at times. I personally experienced a sense of fear and anxiety as I anticipated resistances and actually encountered them. Together we found it exciting to discover again the formation of those early years of trust building. During the presentation they added many human interest stories that reflected some of the steps of development. They took great pride in the fact that the congregation was in no way selective as it sought to meet the needs of persons in those early days and together developed a real sense of community. They remembered those days when they felt themselves becoming an AUTONOMOUS community. INITIATIVE and INDUSTRY turned the community on the near south side into a highly independent people. They shopped in each other's stores. They built each other's houses. Money was loaned freely. Any who met misfortune found adequate resources from a loving and caring community. Many of these people gathered then into a worshipping community. The love and care, however, extended far beyond those who became members of the church. People identified themselves as living in the area of the church. They were hard working "southsiders." The hope of many was that their son or daughter would marry one of their own kind and they often did.

What became painful for many of the present members to accept was the value changes that took place in the early 1930's which caused a major identity shift and realignment of intimacies. There slowly took place a shift from a caring of persons to a pride of goods and services. This resulted in an unusual pride for the community and for the church. Community merchants became highly competitive and sometimes jealous. There developed a pride for the "southside" that became competitive with other places in the city. The fulfillment of that pride for the church was the building of a new building in 1932. It was a beautiful new neo-Gothic building, the "only church in the city that was air cooled." The church trophy case became filled with the symbols of the athletic achievements of those days. There was no doubt that this congregtation was the most idealized and most successful congregation of the denomination in the city. To have achieved all of this at the height of the depression made this congregation the envy of many. They became proud of their own accomplishments. Younger families from the city aligned themselves with this successful congregation. Many of the new businesses and professional people who moved to the city from other communities also came to be a part of this progressive worshipping community. This movement of new leadership families into the worshipping community created a leadership shift. A number of the sons and daughters of the older families found themselves deprived of leadership roles. Additional hurt was experienced as some sons and daughters dated and married the more affluent. There developed an attitude of a college and non-college grouping. By the 1950's the social relationships divided themselves into this pattern. The older membership families identified with and gave support to the new leadership and, yet at the same time, some carried deep feelings about their own lessening of significance. Some of this hurt was still expressed at the time the slides were shown. It was painful to see the members identify with this picture and to confront each other honestly. This was the first time they had had an opportunity to look objectively at what had taken place in their lives so many years ago. Although some had difficulty believing, they were grateful. It was as if they now had been given an opportunity to express the hurt that had been a part of their lives for so many years.

From the time of this original encounter the hard core of resistance in the church has begun to fade, though some is still there. Death of the institution no longer is accepted as something for the near future. By far the largest number have begun to look at their own lives and the life of the church with new affirmation.

As the group continued to view the slides of our most recent years they saw the correlation between their present feelings and Erikson's levels of development of GENERATIVITY vs. STAGNATION and INTEGRITY vs. DESPAIR. It gave me an opportunity to honestly share some of my own feelings of frustration and hurt and to express my own sense of regret for turning to an authoritarian role.

THESE THINGS TOOK PLACE THRU OUR EXPLORATIONS

As the result of this first use of Erikson's model, I became deeply interested in the process of growth and development of persons and institutions in the urban setting. Because of my own personal search and becoming part of a team to strategize for urban ministry, I was asked to teach a course at our denominational seminary. The course was designed for seminary students, pastors and laymen. Ten members of my own church attended the first class. From this we developed with some struggle a strategy for further self-evaluation and direction with the use of the Erikson model.

A questionnaire was sent to every member of the church and, as a result several changes were made in the life and program of the church. The church board held a retreat which included an intensive evaluation of me and a unanimous affirmation of my continuing in the role of pastor. My own shift of attitude in leadership enabled a significant core of laypersons to develop some further strategy completely apart from me. This has resulted in the addition of another pastor to the staff of the church. Together as pastors we have become involved in many forms of creative worship with only the slightest resistance from members of the church. In many instances lay persons have assisted both in the planning and in leading the celebrations. A sanctuary that once was almost solely traditional is now beginning to be the scene of multimedia presentations, dramas, and dialogue dimensions of worship. Banners appear again and again to support particular themes of celebration.

An adjunct person has been added to the staff for counseling purposes. The church has come to sponsor a "Reading is Fundamental" program within the local public school system. Other new programs are now being evaluated such as music training, family counseling and programs for the elderly. Already we have a new group of elderly, called the Mature Moderns, who plan and program their own activities. As pastor, I have a new program of graduate study in Counseling and Personnel. In this program, I will seek to validate through research some of the hypotheses that have emerged through applying the Erikson model to institutional growth and development.

Through a small group·ministry we now have nearly 70 persons sharing their lives together. There is a feeling that the congregation is discovering some new depths of becoming a caring community. The church board has restructured itself into a model designed to more closely correlate needs and tasks. This is being done largely through lay leadership. For most of the church there is now a looking to the future with new feelings of INTEGRITY rather than DESPAIR.

THE DEVELOPMENTAL LIFE STORY OF THIS CONGREGATION AS WE CAME TO UNDERSTAND IT

After and as a result of the showing of the original slide presentation and through the wrestling of the group that attended the seminary classes several conclusions were reached. One was that there was little trust in the life of the total church. Within groups there was some trust, but even this trust was very fragile. Most of the pride of the earlier years was now gone. In its place were only a sense of SHAME and a deep DOUBT that this congregation would ever again become significant. There was a pervasive feeling of GUILT within the church. We should be doing something, but we simply failed to show the INITIATIVE to begin. Those who did were often criticized to the point of giving up. We found ourselves comparing our congregation to others and feeling inferior. The vast shift in values because of social change made it impossible for the church to see itself as a whole. People that used to gather in homes on Sunday evenings were now leaving evening worship to return to their homes alone. With few young people having any part in the life of the church there developed a feeling of STAGNATION. There was only one real conclusion, that under all of our striving for life and renewal we were all experiencing feelings of DESPAIR. Persons who aligned themselves with the pastor for some specific program often became suspected by others. People expressed mistrust in each other. Even more important there was a deep feeling of mistrust that the institution could in any way meet the needs of its individual members. Erikson's model helped us to take some specific steps. Now to take up the sequence of life development.

THE TRUST vs. MISTRUST EXPLORATION

My first step to establish trust was to ask if I could contract with the Adult Class for the original slide presentation. This was a class which was itself quite autonomous. They had their own teacher and existed quite independently from the central life of the church. The retreat of the church board, which is now an annual experience, the congregational questionnaire with visible results of trust building, and a shift in my own attitudes of leadership all have helped to create some new dimensions of trust. Obviously, this was not done without struggle and some mistrust still remains, particularly in the lives of those who previously have risked and been hurt. Equally as important to the sense of a growing trust in each other has been the fact that we have begun to experience some new trust in the institution itself. With a sense of trust as an institution some can begin to say, with Erikson, "I am what I hope I have and give." Given the corporate dimension it has become for us, "We are what we hope we have and give." (Erikson, 1968, p. 107)

AUTONOMY vs. SHAME AND DOUBT EXPLORATION

Through the process of self evaluation the words were expressed again and again, "We need to have a new sense of enthusiasm." It did not take long for those who were involved to understand that enthusiasm cannot be manufactured. Fundamental to the loss of enthusiasm were a lack of a basic sense of purpose and accompanying values. Part of our first consistory retreat was an attempt to draft some basic purposes and to redefine some of the values by which we were seeking to be a worshipping and serving community. We found it was a real struggle to bring into focus some basic purposes which would meet with wide acceptance within the church. There still is division on some basic issues. The process of uniting values was even more difficult. In fact, it has not yet been accomplished at this time. At best we have begun to accept the fact that persons hold differing values and that we will have to live seeking to understand those differing values.

This basically has meant that we have to come to recognize and somewhat accept that we are becoming a heterogenious church reflecting attitudes and values of a wide spectrum of human existence rather than the homogeneous church which once existed on the "southside." As this slowly has become the feeling experienced, some of the membership groups within the church have begun to express a sense of AUTONOMY telling others that there is a community of persons who accept each other even though there exist some differences. In the institutional sense some are beginning to say "We are what we can and will freely." (Erikson, 1968, p. 114) At this time there is only a hope for a broad sense of autonomy in which the whole congregation can experience together.

INITIATIVE vs. GUILT

With new feelings of autonomy, groups within the church are now showing new initiative to move out in behalf of the normative concerns that they hold. Those who are not necessarily a part of a specific program are showing support and often do not hesitate to claim ownership. The Reading Is Fundamental program for instance has received financial support from persons who are not part of the program. In turn, these persons are finding that others within the church are supportive to their particular interests. As a result there has been far fewer expressions of feelings of guilt. If there are, it is basically because our resources at this time do not enable us to take on new involvements. Many are expressing new dreams and often come to the pastor's office to chat about them or openly to express them in planning meetings. In Erikson's words the institution is saying corporately, "We are what we can imagine we will be." (Erikson, 1968, p. 122)

INDUSTRY vs. INFERIORITY

Erikson defines this stage as, "We are what we can learn to make work," (Erikson, 1968, p. 127). It was as we began to take a candid look at our resources both financial and human that we were convinced that our lack of industry was not because of a lack of resources. It was either because we did not use our resources well, or because of a lack of commitment to the purposes and values of the institution. We found we were often choosing the same people again and again to the neglect of others. From the questionnaires and other resources we have begun to discover both the interest and the abilities of our members. With these growing insights we have not hesitated to ask persons to assist. The response has been heartening. We have persons involved in tasks who have never before had an active part in the institutional life of the church. In the process we have sharpened our management and leadership expectations with the confirmed purpose of not wasting the time of our membership on the inconsequential. This has resulted in shorter and fewer planning meetings and more and more direct involvement in ministry. There has been an obviously good feeling of satisfaction from those who have given themselves in the industry of the institution. We have tried to guard ourselves against unrealistic goals and objectives so that we may keep within the reach of the resources that are available to us. As we discover a greater acceptance of mutual trust and purposing we believe there will be experienced a sense of industry in a greater part of the congregation.

IDENTITY vs. IDENTITY DIFFUSION

The real key to a meaningful presence and future of this congregation will be determined by the degree that they will be able to arrive at a new IDENTITY. At present there is more IDENTITY DIFFUSION than IDENTITY FORMATION. Our hope is based on the fact that we have begun to see a change. Many have come to a real awareness that the "southside" IDENTITY is a thing of the past. Some are still trying to carry their present neighborhood IDENTITY back to the neighborhood of the church. On the other hand, there is a growing number of our membership who see themselves as part of the larger city. The city has become their point of reference and the church has become an avenue of ministry for the city. They see themselves as significant persons for the city through their vocations and that sense of significance is beginning also to be felt as they take places of leadership within the church. They are more and more expressing themselves in the corporate first person of "We," (Erikson, 1968, p. 135).

Not until, however, there develops a greater agreement and commitment to normative values and a greater consensus as to our basic purposes will that sense of "We" be strong enough to enable us to say that we have an institutional IDENTITY. Strong and different individual identities and commitments not only continue to block the formation of a corporate identity, but stifle the willingness to risk. However, the very fact that there is a growing awareness of the IDENTITY DIFFUSION is the hope for arriving at a strong institutional IDENTITY.

INTIMACY vs. ISOLATION

Erikson describes this level of development as "We are what we love," (Erikson, 1968, p. 138). In seeking to assess the sense of belonging of the congregation reflected a variety of intimacies both in the personal lives of the church members and in the expectations of what our institutional belongings should be. Many persons who had been very active in the past had retreated into personal isolation. Some, because of extreme hurt as the result of a willingness to risk, found other institutions through which to express themselves. A real effort to have more people become part of the decision making process has helped. The creation of a time for coffee fellowship between the worship and Christian Education hour has brought some new lives in touch with each other. However, these coffees remain largely within a subculture grouping. Once again some families are taking the initiative to share with other families socially. The problem is that most of this intimacy building is also still being done within culture groups of the church. We still hear the cry of those who feel left out and unattended. There is real doubt on behalf of some of the members as to whether we will ever be able to have the kind of intimacy for which some people long. This lack of personal intimacy reflects itself in the institutional dimension of intimacy as well. Only recently have we begun to see signs of persons wanting the church to have a concern for other institutions. The Reading Is Fundamental programs is one example. There are a number of people who are developing a concern for such institutions as our denominational seminary, our schools, both public and private, and some of our local agencies which are seeking to help people. There is expressed by some the same kind of doubt for our institutional intimacies as are expressed for some of the personal intimacies. Our "loves" are divided and no doubt will remain so. However, our determination "to love" has been sharpened. It will appear that we have reached a time when as an institution we will have several "loves" in which only some of the congregation will actively share, but "loves" which hopefully will be supported by the whole of the institution.

GENERATIVITY vs. STAGNATION

This stage of development becomes in Erikson's terms, "We are what we can generate," (Erikson, 1968, p. 138). It is precisely at this level that the shift in pastoral leadership was the most significantly felt. Once the decision was made to shift from a more directly involved role to a role of enabler, new leadership began to emerge. Individuals were encouraged to take risks in new roles of leadership, with some risking to the point of hurt. However, there was experienced an awareness that programs and ideas could be developed without having either the sanction or leadership of the pastor. This was most obviously experienced in the selection and deciding upon a second pastor for the church staff. The group called the Mature Moderns began with just a handful of people and are now completely self determining. The Reading Is Fundamental program is largely led by the lay leadership of the church together with persons from the community.

Part of the motivation for this new generative spirit was the acceptance that we would have to try certain kinds of ministries and accept the fact that some would no doubt fail. Many have come to accept failure not as a negative experience but rather simply as one of the consequences of risk taking. Fundamental to this attitude shift was the shift in the concept formation of institution. No longer does the majority of the congregation think of institutionalizing programs. Rather, we are seeking to institutionalize values. This now allows us to let some programs die and to begin new ones. This of course is very painful for those persons who have invested years in some particular form of ministry or program. It often still causes resistance as we seek to meet human needs through new and creative forms. To what degree we will fully be able to make this transition still will have to be determined. For already we see the temptation to institutionalize some of our new programs. It is my personal conviction that the degree that we will be successful will determine how much generative power we will experience.

INTEGRITY vs. DESPAIR

"We are what survives us," (Erikson, 1968, p. 139) is the descriptive feeling that Erikson uses for this final stage of development. Through the eleven years of my pastorate I have seen a dramatic shift in the attitudes of those of the congregation who are 70 years plus. The imminence of their own personal death has brought about a new feeling about the institution. Most of those of this age would certainly hope that the institution of the church would continue. However, they now are beginning to see that the worth of their past years of investment is not determined by whether or not this specific institution survives. Rather they look for a survival of their values in persons, including those who have been part of this institution but have now found themselves involved in other church and community institutions. This is not true of the younger members, particularly those in their middle years. As a result there is still a motivation for survival for this particular church behind much of their support for new programs and their willingness to look for new directions. Therefore, I anticipate that those who have this present attitude will experience a sense of DESPAIR from time to time as they experience a sense of bleakness about the future of the church. Those who see hope only in return to past forms will no doubt experience despair and voice it often. Some already act out this DESPAIR by inactivity or by aggressively challenging the leadership of the church. Some express hope only through a change of leadership. It remains to be seen to what degree the church as a whole will be able to experience a sense 'of INTEGRITY about its future. Perhaps there will have to be a shift of leadership and programming. However, it would appear that these changes will not significantly affect any sense of INTEGRITY until the congregation can experience as a whole the other preceding levels of development beginning with BASIC TRUST.

CONCLUSION

To sum up what I believe is happening both for me and the congregation — we have simply stopped long enough in our own processing to take an honest look at what was happening to ourselves. Erikson's model was helpful, not primarily as a token of measurement, but as a cognitive instrument whereby a group of people could identify their own stages of development within a process of institutional development. We have come to see ourselves as a developmental process. We have found that we can reach backward with meaning and forward with hope once we discover the meaning of our lived moments of frustration. I believe that the fundamental premise of our effort — that groups (in this case a congregation) have a personality and a developmental process that is similar to individual persons — is very productive.

How a Church began with a Childrens' Choir

BY FRAZIER N. ODOM
Faith Lutheran Church

*"We've come this far by faith,
Leaning on the Lord;
Trusting in His holy Word ......
He's never failed me yet ...... "*

At 10:45 a.m. each Sunday morning a group of young souls intone these words as they glide single-file down the aisle of Faith Lutheran church. They are youthful, vibrant personalities; sparking a dynamic lived moment. In a church where the rubrics are often so restrictive and prohibitive; where the liturgy is so low-keyed and expressionless, even the most reserved worshipper must admit the presence of the SPIRIT OF THE LIVING GOD!

The story you are about to hear is their story. It is the story of lives...human lives...reaching out to touch the lives of other human beings; a story of spirited young people (now teenagers, for the most part) who banded together to use their voices to the glory of their God and the subsequent development of a worshipping, believing, Spirit-filled community.

I would not have this story to tell were it not for one individual. It is a beautiful, warm-hearted person whose unbelievable patience and obsession with children makes me proud to call her my wife. In a sense, this is her story as well as the childrens'. Very shortly you shall see why.

The story has its beginning in the turbulent year of 1968. America was at war in Laos, Cambodia and Viet Nam. Mass protests and demonstrations pervaded the land. Moral decadence and spiritual upheavals tested the life and vitality of the Christian faith. Martin Luther King was assassinated. Scores of major cities in the United States were experiencing the effects of Black consciousness and the expanding ghetto tested the mission affirmations and convictions of mainline denominations and congregations. Reconstructions and the will-to-be-the-church prevailed in some places; racism, fear, panic and evacuation prevailed in others.

It was no different here in Chicago. There were still those who were faintly saying "hold the line at 79" (alluding to holding Blacks north of 79th Street). The wall did not hold. Blacks began moving into Foster Park, into Auburn Park and on into Gresham.

83rd and Sangamon, in the Gresham area, is the locale of this story. Faith Lutheran Church is situated here. In 1968, an all-white congregation of 500 plus, wrestled with its mission to a changing community. It is one of the many that failed to make the right decision. The whole story is an horrendous one. Suffice it to say that the congregation dropped from 500 plus in one week to 69 the next. Blacks in the community had been ignored. Black children who attempted to visit the church for Sunday School were turned away. Black adults who dared to come to the worship service, were treated as though they did not exist. In effect, the community was turned off.

When I arrived in Chicago in the summer of 1968 with my wife and four young children the prospects looked gloomy. I had 69 elderly whites from the original congregation to work with......no Blacks! It was frightening! With a stigma on the church ("they didn't want us there then, why do they want us now?"), coupled with expressed hostility toward me as a Black person working with "white racists" in a German church, and a ridiculously low-budget, the problem looked insurmountable. The anguish in my wife was most evident. Perhaps I should have stayed in Selma, Alabama, I thought.

The first rays of hope emanated from the children...ours and others in the community. Here children would gather to play. For whatever reasons (and I could think of some) parents did not seem to mind so much about their children coming to play with ours. Whatever animosity they as parents had for the church as a symbol, or us as suspected condoners of that activity, the feelings seemed to fade when it came to the children.

It dawned on my wife and me that children have a natural knack of drawing children. And if there is anything our children have ever been good for doing it's just that...drawing other children. They had everything in their favor: the space, the equipment and the willingness. It was not all without bother, to be sure. Here a broken window, there a hole where some child decided to play groundhog, and various fisticuffs and scrimmages. Taken together, we determined that the children were pretty naughty. It was in the backyard, which served as the local "park", that my wife and I discovered an entry into ministry. The children, we figured, would be the best route of getting into the hearts and homes of parents.

In those days of summer, 1968, we had the opportunity to invite parents to visit our church whenever they would come looking for their offspring. Ironically, the parents almost always expected their children to be with our children. When they were not, there was disappointment. It seemed to them that if they were anywhere else they "were in trouble, or had no business being gone." Our invitations would be met with polite "maybes," but no promises. Nothing happened. We changed our strategy and asked the parents to let us have their children to begin a Sunday school. They would promise to think about it. Still, we had no children other than our own: a four-child Sunday School!

It was not until the summer of 1969 that we got the first three children (other than our own) to come to Sunday School on a regular basis. A breakthrough! Others followed ... then others. Soon we had twenty-five ... then thirty ... then forty. We solicited the aid of two other people from another congregation to assist us in the Sunday School training. Our emphasis during the year 1969 was to teach songs to the children in hopes of interesting them in making up a choir for whatever service we could conduct with the few whites who made up the membership.

Feedback from those involved in the early group indicate that they persuaded their parents to let them come to our Sunday School. They liked to sing! Slowly, parents began to trust us; to feel comfortable with us. They gradually gave their permission to let my wife have them on Friday evenings for choir practices. They loved this. The parents, it seems, could have cared less. (I, perhaps, could deduce reasons for this, also.) The children looked forward to each Friday's rehearsal, and, as you may imagine, came early for preliminary play. Other children who, either because they were reluctant or did not have the blessings of their parents to participate, would gather at the door and the windows of the church to observe what their peers were doing. We knew they wanted to participate but we were powerless to do anything about it. We never would deny the "outsiders" any of the goodies that the choir children enjoyed. Very often we observed all of the children (choir as well as "outsiders") singing the songs. They all knew the songs equally as well. Yet, we had only six that were called by the early choir name, "Tiny Tots."

This early sextet looked forward to singing on Sunday mornings with great anticipation and enthusiasm. Simple songs they would be to the general public, but to them they were classics. Songs like "Jesus Loves Me," and "Gentle Jesus, Meek and Mild" sounded forth from them with great effort and pride.

Something else was happening that we know all along was bound to happen. My wife was being criticized by the white membership for the loudness of the childrens' singing; for their behavior in the choir stand. The inference had a great impact upon us. The second exodus of whites began toward the latter stages of 1969. Membership decreased; attendance waned. We were quite sure that our effort had gone for naught. Few Black adults attended. The pressure once more became almost unbearable from a personal and mission board standpoint. Had the ministry at Faith congregation failed? Would the church have to close down completely? Would the Pastor and his wife have to tell these little ones that the building would have to be sold; that he would have to leave with his wife and four children? I was not above crying; I did!

My reports to the mission board were pitiful, to say the least. They deal in statistics, and I had none. My little congregation was losing members instead of gaining. In fact, there was not yet one baptized child on the roll. It seemed hopeless. I argued and pleaded with the mission board to let me continue to work at Faith. My point was that my wife and I had a hunch that it was more feasible to try to work with the young children first, in order to get to the parents. I argued that in this situation it would be easier to work toward gaining the young in order to let the young interest, convince, motivate the parents. The arguments seemed futile, for the board was concerned about financing.....$30,000 worth of financing, and no adults to help pick up the slack. With much reluctance and skepticism, the board allowed our mission to continue.

The hunch began to pay off in 1970. The Sunday School increased; the choir increased; and Black adults came into the church much more rapidly as whites departed. One would surmise that the reason Black adults came into the church is the vacating of all whites. This is logical, but not true. The truth of the matter is that fathers and mothers, influenced by the children and interested in seeing and knowing what their children were doing, decided that this was for them. Their children were pushing to be baptized, and parents figured it would be best for all to be at one place.

Akin to the notion of children influencing their parents is the fact that as Pastor I never emphasized Lutheranism, but Christianity. I always said that I was interested in building a community of believers. The children followed this line of thinking and began to create, innovate and do their own thing with songs. Now the choir was called the youth choir.

1971 to 1973 produced even more adults and children. There were no whites left. The mission board took the credit for the success. The choir became the young adult choir during the period and raised monies to buy its first robes. The entire service was centered around the children. The music progressed from the more traditional music (anthems and hymms) to Gospel. This resonated as much with the membership as it did the youth. There was that anticipation of the choir singing, especially following one of the laboriously difficult gregorian chants of the hymnbook. Clapping was introduced in the service. The swaying of the youth as they sang brought new life and joy and enthusiasm to the worshippers.

The years from 1974 to date have been the most spectacular in terms of the choir's effect upon the church and its growth. More members have joined, and, in most instances, the parents have followed soon thereafter. There has never been a case at Faith when a whole family unit has come into the membership at one time. It has ALWAYS been after the children have expressed a "liking" or a willingness "to belong" that the parents have joined.

During these latter years, the choir has embarked upon doing things in an ecumenical way. This is indicative of what we have tried to tell them about being Christians first. They have periodic concerts with the others of various denominations; they sing in other churches; and they volunteer to participate. They do not call what they are doing being "ecumenical", however. They call it sharing and learning: sharing themselves as a group which has confidence in what it is doing, and learning how others do songs to either imitate or improvise.

A few weeks ago the choir members came to me en masse and said, "We don't want to be called Young Adult Choir anymore. We're the Faith Lutheran Young Adult Concert Choir." They made sure it was printed that way in the next Sunday's bulletin.

You see, without these young people, teenagers now, it would have hardly been possible for Faith Lutheran Church to have gotten off the ground and recovered from those hectic days of 1968. Space and time just do not allow me the luxury of telling you all of the glorious things I could say about this bunch of God's people. This much I can offer you as living testimony. Let the people who have come into Faith Lutheran Church tell you how they got there:

One says: "Frankly, I came because I love to hear the children sing ..... this church is close by . ... and they inspire me."

Another says: "Pastor, you're terrific, but when my child started talking so much about how he wanted to be with the others in the choir, that turned my husband and I on to becoming members."

Yet another says: "I heard so much about Mrs. Odom. When I met her I knew my child was in good company. You're really blessed!"

The testimonies could go on and on, but the real tribute, as you see, belongs to the children who formed a choir. Were you a member of the 275 at Faith today, and of the scores who have come through Faith and are now in other places, the chances are 50-50 that you came as a result of the influence of the choir.

But the choir is more than just **a** choir. By that I do not mean to insinuate that it is extraordinary (in the popular use of the term) but that it is a fraternity. Its members are devoted to mutual respect and Christian love. Discipline and faithfulness are hallmarks of excellence, and anyone who shirks practice will not be expected to show up for a singing engagement. No one is excluded, including pianist, or director. It is a peer counseling group. They share each other's problems and offer advice of the highest quality. Whenever they are in doubt about an issue, the Pastor is always contacted. There is no "boss" within the group, even though there are a couple who stubbornly claim the title.

It has not always been so good with the group. Things got rather rocky during the past three years, but that has passed over. There was a time when petty rivalries for lead singer of a particular song, threatened to divide the group; other times when squabbles took place for no apparent reason. Led to see its role in the church, and reminded constantly of its contribution to the birthing of the church, the choir has arrived.

The choir has some other things for which to be proud. It has sparked within the last two years another Tiny Tot group which will one day take its place. A male chorus has been started; also, a Senior Choir. Very frequently the Young Adult Concert Choir will join the Senior Choir in a rendition, and teach the Senior Choir how to clap...and sway...and, yes...to sing out!

The day will soon some when this choir that helped build a church will fade from the scene. It will be not because of tension or disharmony, but because of the places they will have to take in the world. Some will be getting married in the near future. Others will move off to colleges to seek vocations in the world. Whatever the case, age and time will take them from the seats they occupy so faithfully every Sunday.....if no other place than the Senior Choir. 70% of them have come the entire journey from Tiny Tot to Youth Choir to Young Adult and now to the Faith Lutheran Young Adult Concert Choir.

I only pray that they will take with them the learning instilled in them by my wife and me; that they will maintain their belief in Jesus Christ as Lord.

Yes, it is true that,

> "They've come a long way by faith,
> leaning on the Lord;
> Trusting in His holy Word......
> He's never failed them yet....."

.....On they move down the aisle of Faith Lutheran Church, swinging, smiling; yet intent and sincere.....There's Cherry playing the piano; Daryl on the drums; and Andrea and Laverne directing.....Tarsha and Monique, the youngest and smallest ...... Jonathan ...... Ina ...... Ronald ...... Pam ...... Eric ...... Cheryl ...... John ...... Alicia ...... Dino ...... Sharon ...... Paula ...... Barry ...... Kimberly ...... Ingrid ...... Torrence ...... on and on they come. But these are the ones who know HOW A CHURCH WAS BUILT WITH A CHILDRENS' CHOIR.

Ministry of the Aging Through A Congregation

By THOMAS H. EVANS

I am the pastor of a United Church of Christ in Whitewater, Wisconsin, located just two blocks from Fairhaven, a United Church retirement home. More than a third of our congregation of 530 is made up of persons who have reached or even far exceeded retirement age. Since beginning my pastorate in Whitewater four years ago, I have continuously shared with the congregation a deep concern for the life journey of these older members. Sometimes by careful planning, and often by spontaneous response to one another, our congregation has been creating an enterprise of significant meaning which fully incorporates the ministry of these people, with surprising results. A critical incident may serve to illustrate.

On October 31, 1976, our congregation celebrated "Fairhaven Sunday" with a unique service of worship designed to give recognition to the contributions made by the Fairhaven Community and the many gifts which are shared through our church by **all** older people in the community. It was to be seen as a concrete example of the church's ministry with and for all older people. The order of worship alone listed 60 persons directly involved in these ministries, the vast majority of them over 65 years of age!

Our worship that morning was divided into three segments, each of them an important symbolic part of the shared ministry between church and retirement home. In the first part, held in the church worship center, we shared in a rather traditional service in which the liturgical parts were led by older perons. The Prelude and Offertory were played in duet by our regular younger organist on the organ and piano. The anthem was sung by the Fairhaven Chorus, composed of twenty residents of the home, most of them lifelong choir members now retired. The Pastoral Prayer was written and given by a retired lady who had been a deaconness in a large church for many years. The Mission Moment, stating the gratitude of the church for the State Conference's work in health and welfare institutions, was prepared and given by an older lady who had served in conference work herself, and knew those commitments intimately. Highlight of the service was a "Sermon in Sight and Sound" (slide/audio cassette) entitled "The Throwaway Generation." It was written and produced by a retired United Church minister who had originally created it for a photography class taken the year before in a senior citizen's project at our local state university campus.

The second part of the liturgy moved the congregation outdoors. Donning hats and coats, men, women and children exited by the church east door to gather around the Fairhaven Community Van. The President of the Whitewater City Council, a Roman Catholic layman and a member of the Van Advisory Committee, there led the people in a short litany of dedication for the van, recently put into service for all elderly and handicapped persons in Whitewater. This dedication was then closed with a prayer by the Fairhaven chaplain.

In the third part, the congregation walked hand in hand to Fairhaven, and there shared in an anniversary celebration (the 19th). We met and heard from two of the first residents at Fairhaven, joined in a thanksgiving prayer, and closed the entire liturgy with a benediction by the minister. We then remained for the accustomed "coffee hour," only this time in the setting of an anniversary party featuring a special cake, a beautiful display of arts and crafts by residents, and of course a congenial host of people who welcomed us to their home.

Fairhaven Sunday was not unlike the special worship occasions and celebrations which dot the calendar of your local church. It was successful in that it involved a much larger group of people in planning and leadership than usual, provided some creative change in worship format, and stimulated the interest of the whole congregation in lifting up a special focus of life and witness which was directly related to their personal experience.

That Sunday celebration symbolized a faith stance about aging which the church desperately needs to share as it moves rapidly into the last decades of a century in which the latter years of life have become a major agenda item for the entire society. In its own small way, Fairhaven Sunday brought to celebrative focus a whole series of intitiatives in our congregation to change the prevalent views about older people in churches.

It is abundantly clear today that our society has awakened mightily to the needs and concerns of its older citizens - not only to their physical and material needs, but to their emotional, psychological and spiritual needs as well. The wealth of material now being produced in every form of print and electronic media about aging; the local, state, and federal monies now being invested in aging projects (witness our own Fairhaven Van); and the emerging sensitivity about use of language and the arts in dealing with aging are sufficient indicators of this immense enterprise in changing consciousness and behaviour. Such initiatives are long awaited and much welcomed. Yet there remain many subtle stumbling blocks to societal reform and new direction in dealing with older persons, not least of which are intransigent attitudes and assumptions which still go unquestioned. And many of those attitudes, wittingly or unwittingly, are being maintained and even fostered in the church.

Let's look at a few rather typical samples:
a) "Old people in the church want things to remain the same. They want to sing the old hymns, worship the way they always have, and keep things

on an even keel, come what may. They are basically against change, and one needs to be careful with them when introducing new ideas."

b) "A church with an older membership is in trouble. Everyone knows that youth are abandoning the church, and when they are gone, the church will die with the older people."

c) "It is really older people who kill some of our large churches. They refuse to change with the times, they tie up the church purse strings, they won't welcome new residents in the neighborhood, and so the church slowly strangles to death and dies."

d) "Old people in the church have 'served their time.' They have raised their families, helped in the Sunday School, served on the boards and in the Women's Fellowship, and now they want and deserve rest. You can't expect too much from them."

Such images contain just enough truth to be powerfully influential in the life of the church. In fact they are powerful enough to be dangerous in their implications for older people.

We need to give testimony against such images out of live situations which demonstrate creative options which negate them. We need to work on serious alternatives, because such images are in fact images of death, in a community of faith that emphatically and regularly espouses options of Christian life and vitality.

Let me present some options that we believe in.

I.

Old people want things to remain the same. One has to be careful with them when introducing new ideas.

Fortunately or unfortunately, we are finding that you have to be careful with **all** people in introducing change. None of us like radical change which directly affects us, unless it offers some valued dimension of life. And older people, given a chance to understand the values being offered can be powerfully affirming of change and innovation. In fact they have a rare capacity for leading the forces of change, given the right opportunity.

In our congregation we have introduced a whole series of new initiatives in worship, education, and mission, publicized them well, explained the rationale for doing them, and then carried them out. An alive jazz liturgy featuring the "Celebration Road Show" brought together the young people of the Wisconsin Conference UCC and our members in the church worship center. The service built up emotional momentum until it achieved a climactic ending which issued in spontaneous snake dances in the aisles, enthusiastic foot-stomping and hand clapping, and a kind of singing more often associated with the revival meeting than the typically staid congregational-style monotone. Our "older" congregation not only liked it; they thought it was the best service they had ever attended!

A retired organist, trained in the theatre organ tradition which began with accompaniment of silent movies and circus performances, helped organize and present a series of popular organ concerts in the church on

Sunday afternoons. His musical fare featured everything from "Begin the Beguine" to an original score for accompaniment of the 1923 silent film, "King of Kings" by Cecil B. DeMille. The vast majority of those attending regularly had gray hair!

A Bicentennial worship service featuring Communion with brown bread and Madeira wine - the minister, congregational moderator, and song leader in striking costumes - and a whole series of congregational exercises in prayer and praise elicited strong affirmation from all attending, including our older members.

Why these responses? Because people were well-informed; because no one assumed **anyone** was against appropriate change or had to be treated "carefully" — that is, by covert manipulation behind the scenes. It was our older membership that gave the strongest affirmation, who asked for more variety and experimentation, and who took most delight in the evidence of new spirit in the church. Many affirmed change because they knew from years of experience that change was most often helpful. Others expressed gratitude for continuing variety in the church's expression and demonstration of faith, admitting that their own daily routines had become terribly boring and therefore deeply frustrating. Others, valuing efforts to invite an influx of younger people into the church circles saw it as an appropriate way to reach them, and affirmed that.

II.

A church with an older membership is in trouble. The church will die with its older people.

Our older members bring a richness of experience and wisdom in ministry which is unsurpassed. From those deeply rooted in the Whitewater community, and from those who have served sacrificially for many years in other communities and have finally chosen to spend their later years in a church home in our community, our church receives gift upon gift in Christian commitment and witness. A predecessor worship service to Fairhaven Sunday, called "Older's Sunday," celebrated those gifts, much as we celebrate the gifts of young people each year on the traditional Children's Day. One of our organ concerts occasioned an art display in the church parlor by an older lady who does watercolors and acrylics. The Women's Fellowship was so impressed with her work that they bought a number of them, had them framed and hung permanently in that same parlor. A retired dean of the Chicago Law School, and a prominent national Episcopal churchman served as chairman of the statewide ecumenical campus ministry, and still acts as consultant to the local campus ministry board. A retired UCC minister served a few hours each week as Visitation Minister for the church, and taught adult education courses on Sundays during the same period. Several retired church members, trained teachers and nurses, serve voluntarily with the public schools in tutoring and counseling. And the listing of such Christian work goes on and on.

Is it sufficient to say that older people are dying at the same rate as everyone else? Or more importantly, that death interrupts the creative offering of individual lives whenever it comes? It is a question of images, and a question of our choice of life-giving and life-sustaining alternatives. No wonder that the motto of that church retirement home reappears in our local enterprise again and again: the motto: **Where Life is Added to Years.**

III.

But we must hasten on, and our list of crippling images is no longer than the testimonies all of us could offer as life-giving alternatives.

"Older people tie up the church purse strings." (An alternate form of that image: all older pople are on fixed income and can't afford to do much).

Our church recently pledged and paid more than $10,000 for the United Church 17/76 Achievement Fund Drive, to aid black colleges in the South and overseas educational ministries. A substantial amount of that money, including the largest single pledge, came from older people. One wants to ask: who inquired of those retired people what they really **cared** about? To what they wished to give sacrificially. We could hardly believe the response. There is a limit to such resources — granted. But there is surprising power in those resources when people choose to use them in the ministry of Jesus Christ.

IV.

Old people have served their time; they want and deserve rest.

Many of our members cannot teach in the church school or serve on the church boards; many are housebound and in wheelchairs; many are lost in the sad wilderness of senility. Endless literature quantifies the failing capacities and abilities of aging folk. Yet again the question is not whether many will minister, but whether an appropriate form of ministry is offered. A group of our church members at Fairhaven collect and crush tin cans in the kitchen each week to support the recycling effort; several ladies who cannot get out often any longer assist as parish phone visitors, recruit Sunday greeters, or lead devotions for others less fortunate than themselves. The Fairhaven van helps many continue to shop for themselves. It is a federally funded project initiated by the expressed need of older people as an outreach mission of Fairhaven for the whole community, brought to being through the expertise of the Fairhaven administrator/chaplain who knew what it took to find and corral the appropriate funding and organization.

One lady rides the van quite regularly. She rides, not because she needs to — but in order to assist the more than 40 volunteer drivers in operation of the van and in finding street names and addresses. She has lived in Whitewater all her life; she knows every street.

The image of rest is appropriate for many older people, but not as an image of **ending**, of death. Physical and mental incapacity are a fact for many older people, but they do not determine the spirit by which the people need and wish to **live**.

CONCLUSION

An earlier observation noted the immense enterprise of our society in changing consciousness and behaviour regarding aging people. If there is an overarching Christian conviction which motivates this paper, it is that too much of that enterprise is concerned with what society and the church is to do **to** and **for** older people, instead of **with** and **alongside them**. If Christians affirm that the ultimate purpose of the Christ-like life is to give of oneself as an act of devotion to God — to be fundamentally **for others**, then our ministry must be ministry **of** the aging in our congregations, not something different or less.

Active, Potent, Desirable Minister for Now: A Dialogue

ROY LARSON and ROSS SNYDER

Snyder: Roy Larson is the religious editor of the **Sun Times**, and he and I have known each other for some time. We worked together on a young adult project in the United Methodist Church some 15-20 years ago, and every once in a while he calls by telephone or comes out and talks. We agreed that we would just sit here and talk about something we wanted to talk about.

Roy, we're talking about image a great lot this week, and I am culling my brain each time to come up with a compelling image that those of us here will never forget. From your running around this country and observing, how would you describe an active, potent, desirable minister for the 1970's.

Larson: I think in the 8 years that I've been on this job, the religious person who has made the deepest impression on me has been Abraham Joshua Heschel. I remember his saying one time that the distinguishing mark of the man of faith is . . . "**audacity**." As I understand it, audacity has something to do with the beatitude "Blessed are the pure in heart," which has something to do with singleness of heart. When there's this kind of coherence in an individual's life, he or she is capable of audacity.

A couple of weeks ago I was doing a piece on the United Methodist Church and suggested that the thing which most characterized the bureaucracy of that church was what I called "**unbridled prudence**." A long way from audacity. But if I were looking for the qualities that make for a potent minister, I think I would start there and see where it goes.

Snyder: Do you have any clues about what makes possible audacity?

Larson: Purity of heart, as I understand it, is to will one thing. When your insides are freed from the conflicting elements and your eye is on the target. If you have this quality of singleness of heart, then all of a sudden you become capable of all kinds of things.

Snyder: Are you partly talking about double-mindedness in which one part of your mind is thinking about how people are thinking about what you are doing (and how to digest their opposition) and another part of your mind is trying to invent what you want to do. Being an active, potent, desirable minister requires some way of getting rid of that double-mindedness?

Larson: Precisely. Following Dante's old dictum about going on your own way and letting the people talk. Doing the things a person is required to do in the situation and not measuring, calculating every single consequence. At the same time without being absolutely stupid. There's something to be said for counting the cost too, but you can count the cost and still take the risk.

Snyder: Some people today feel that this singlemindedness is quite dependent upon an outbreaking of pentecostal experience. That single-mindedness comes because there's such a surging of spirited existence within you that you are no longer a divided self. One of the celebrated preachers at the close of the 19th century preached that it's the explosive power of great affection that cures the divided self. Singlemindedness does tend to form of surging up of spirited consciousness; other people's criticism is secondary.

Larson: I think I first learned about the importance (and lack) of singlemindedness when I was in the process of trying to help my church build a building. I remember one climatic evening when we were trying to decide on the design. We had chosen as the central concept to govern the architecture that a congregation is a family of God, and church is a household of faith, the family of God. And what does a family do? It doesn't sit in classrooms or auditoriums in rows; it gathers around the table for a meal. So that was our working concept. And as a result of this, the architect designed a building that was round, a combination of circles and triangles. The congregation bought the concept. But there was one man in the congregation who was hesitant about what people would think of the building. As people of the village went down to the Loop on the train each day and looked at this strange thing, what would they say? And so he said, "why don't we keep the concept, but instead of having the thing round on the outside, square it off."

Well, let the outward man and the inward man be at one. Do the building that says what you want to say. And then some people will hate it. Some people will love it. But nobody will ignore it.

Snyder: Amen.

Larson: But you're not going out calculatedly to shock. Or calculatedly to please. In the old Bonhoefferian terms, faithfulness is the criterion.

Then let what happens, happen. But not try to manipulate and to control the response of other people. That violates their otherness. Then you not only are confronting them with something, you're telling them how they're supposed to respond to it. I don't think you have any right to do that. The work goes on, and the Holy Spirit determines what the response is going to be.

Snyder: One of the new developments that theological education today is trying to bring off is the so-called continued education of ministers. Sometimes I wonder if that isn't a nice, slippery path to the place down below. I wonder if the basic assumption is that if only ministers have a little more education, they won't need the audacity that you're talking about. Do you see any way that continuing education of the minister in getting a doctoral degree could be an opportunity for growth in audacity? (and I'd like to say "Skilled audacity," because you emphasized you don't want to go out and get knocked off just because of some silly stupidity). Buying your point of audacity rather than unbridled prudence, what does that mean for the goals and methods of continuing education of ministers?

Larson: When it gets right down to it, many of the D.Min. programs have one basic objective — not growth in grace as the catalogues say but filling up empty classrooms in the seminaries. They're designed to satisfy the institution's needs, not the needs of the clients. So long as that is taking place, there's going to be a demonic force at work in the programs.

When it comes down to the minister's motivation for getting this degree, too often a dominant force is the way that's going to look on the church bulletin. It's not going to hurt your professional career.

Now if there's anything that will kill audacity, God knows it's careerism. Read **The Gamesman** (it's the new "in thing"). Translate it into ecclesiastical language, and you find it very revealing.

Snyder: Give us an illustration that might make that clearer to us?

Larson: Like me many of the people in this room were going to a seminary in the 1950's in the era of the Organization Man. And that was a dull period, my friends. And the Gamesman, who is the 1970's equivalent of the Organization Man, is somewhat more interesting a creature than the Organization Man because . . .

Snyder: He's more complex?

Larson: Yes. The Gamesman is working in the new technocratic bureaucracy. And things in those fields move so incredibly fast that the old style Company Man is not the kind of man that you want to handle those firms. It requires someone capable of greater audacity than the Company Man or the prudential careerist. It requires a person capable of taking risks. The Gamesman has his problems too. Audacity as some sort of isolated virtue can't be made into an icon. It has to be linked to other things.

A Professional Team

BY CHARLES L. BURNS
Conference Minister
Florida Conference, United Church of Christ.

Can a team of professionally competent peers operate as a Conference Staff? How do you develop such a team? What is the educational model that operates if such a team is possible? As a Conference Minister, how do you model out such an adventure knowing from experience the number of hours you have spent resolving multiple staff conflicts within local churches?

Over the years I have had experiences as a local church pastor with members of Conference Staffs; I have served on Conference Staffs; and, have served as Conference Minister. Given this variety of experience, at times I feel the task of creating such a team to be almost impossible. Still I have had enough good and rewarding experiences as a member of responsible teams to know it can be done and, when achieved, its rewards are multiple. The other reality I face is the truth embodied within the Christian Faith of a covenant community of persons with a variety of gifts - all gifts being necessary for bodily growth. (Ephesians 4)

If you had it would you know it? We often are so consumed with everyday tasks and demands that we fail to recognize the experience of a creative team until after it is gone. I've often said to another, "What fun it was to work with you back then," to hear the reply, "You forget all the problems we had!" Memory does lessen pain, but pain and struggle after result in the most creative and fulfilling experiences.

In retrospect the persons with whom I have most fully experienced fulfillment as a team have shared at least the following:
1. They embody "the message" in their life-styles. They are what they say!
2. They have competency - they are skilled in what they do.
3. A real sense of humanness is primary. The issues of justice and caring come forward.
4. If it's worth doing, they find every way to make it happen. Failure is the opportunity to try again. They are not afraid to risk.
5. They know they cannot do it alone. Others are empowered with energy and skill to fulfill the common goal.

RECRUITMENT

Offering the invitation to another to become a part of a team venture is most difficult. The giver and the gift are a part of all participants. The one who does the inviting becomes the invited, for there is an entering-into a common adventure which continues to change with the addition of another and the fact that experience is always changing. As a Conference Minister I have discovered very little help in the usual denominational profiles for placement. The profile gives needed statistics, plus what friends think. Over the years I've seen too many excellent profiles about individuals with whom I have had too much experience. You wonder if it is the same person.

Unfortunately the advice and recommendations of your peers is not too helpful (with a few grateful exceptions). Conference placement personnel are caught in the middle and hope the Holy Spirit will solve the problems of the minister recommended to another Conference. We pass on problems rather than solve them. Candidates for placement also try to fit themselves into the opportunity, whether they have the desired or expected skills. A certain amount of over-selling is desirable as long as the person can grow and fulfill the need. The biggest problem in team building is the discovery that one who said he can - cannot!

Quite often if committees are involved in the staff recruiting, I note a heavy preference for the fatherly pastoral image. (This is true of many ministers who serve on such committees.) Too often such a pastoral type is limited only to political relational skills, while his degree of professional competency is low. After a short while the good guy image is not enough. Ministers and laity want and deserve specific competent help from their Conference Staff.

I hesitate to print and circulate "Job Descriptions", for too often the invitation becomes the ego-mirror for the candidate. The candidate then "seems" to be one truth, when in reality authenticity is prostituted. Job descriptions often become straitjackets and excuses for the insecure team member. Jobs change; people change; and no one can fully describe the job offered other than in the broadest categories. Personally, the hardest task I face in team building is the researching, searching and inviting of persons to join a team. Consultation with others on the team is helpful (not necessarily right). Interviews with the nominee point towards possibility, but you never know what gifts or weaknesses you have within your team until they are tested.

GOING ABOUT THE TASK

With the addition, loss or change of membership the entire team experiences adjustment. Things will never be as they were. So —
1. Help the remaining staff prepare for change. The initial response is one of rigidity and status quo. They need to know what's happening. Their sense of life space is threatened.
2. Have Standard Operating Procedures in writing to help the new member get on board. Personnel policy manuals or fiscal policy procedures that affect all assist in the process.

The new team constellation needs time to settle into a new style. The first two or four months of staff change involve periods of testing and trying out. I try to keep staff assignments as flexible as possible. Most beginnings are in one-to-one conversation with a minimum of total staff assignments. The more experienced staff personnel must take care of institutional maintenance until the newest member begins to discover his/her place of entry and assignment. All members of the existing staff team have the responsibility for care and nurture of the new addition. (Staff reduction is an entirely different trauma.)

New beginnings call for new settings. Following the introductory phase, the new staff needs to be together in a neutral situation (retreat center) long enough to talk through relationships. If you don't feel right about each other no amount of planning or process newsprint will make much difference. A third party participant observer is often helpful in such a two or three day session. Such a role clarifies feelings and assists team building. Regular longer term staff building experiences are crucial for morale and futuring opportunities.

TO BE PART OF A TEAM

1. Is an **experience of interdependence.** You know your gift is needed - your talent makes a difference - you know if you don't do your homework and carry your share of assignments that others know you've let them down. You can't fake it with your peers. They see through your petty excuses and reasons to the reality that you didn't do what was expected. Too many team failures point the way towards termination and separation. Any competent professional can bluff through a few times, but in a team situation you better not kid yourself - you are known - and you better admit it.

2. Is to **share in planning.** All members have to know where they are going and how together they can assist the process of achievement. All members are planners. For one on the team to be "the planner" is a cop-out on evaluation and performance. Too often do I experience skilled process planners who feel their only job is to assist the others do their work. Such a staff role to me is phony and a way to avoid total team fulfillment. Planning - execution - and evaluation are all part of the assignment. We share together as visionary - planner - enabler - doer - and evaluator. You cannot plan for another. You can help the other with their plans, but it then has to be their vision - their plan - their ability - their evaluation. Personally I think today's "Planner" is a phony unless all parts of the assignment are integrated.

3. Is to **share in leadership.** Leadership is not assigned; it is earned. Leadership changes as role and function change. Every member of the team has to assume and earn a leadership role within the group. As Conference Minister I know I'm not always the leader of our Staff Team. Other levels of experience and ability respond to need, and leadership rotates. The longer a team is together the more often leadership rotates. Different leadership styles and skills strengthen the team. Symbolic of our need to share leadership is the rotating assignment given to each staff member to take his/her turn conducting our regular (bi-monthly) twenty-four hour staff meetings. To be a member of our Staff Team is to be a leader.

4. Is to **risk failure.** To play it cautious or safe is not the climate for team building. You have to know that you are as respected for your obvious failures as you are for any achievement. Staffs grow as they assist

each other towards attainable goals. If we fail to attain we learn what additional skill or growth is needed. To repeat again and again the tried and true is dull and boring. If one is not stretching and occasionally failing then I get the feeling I've a lazy team member. The team has to create the climate of open risk. Judgment is to assist learning, not to punish effort. Every team member strives to assist the other towards joyous fulfillment.

GROWING PAINS IN TEAM BUILDING

Busyness is no excuse for productivity. I've noticed that when a person is not sure what to do he/she sure does a lot of everything - travel here - then travel there - attend this meeting - then go to that meeting. Staff members have to plan their time and know what needs to be done. Just to be present is not enough. (I note many Campus Ministers, not knowing what to do or their function, speak of a "Ministry of Presence.")

Building a fan club is always a staff temptation. We all need ego support, but to always require and seek support from the same persons causes me to wonder.

Giving of favors is a temptation sometimes related to the fan club. Certain persons often receive subsidies for trips or fringe benefits. If such is a result of productivity or the benefit enhances productivity then I have no problem. But I like to ask, "What difference did the special trip or event contribute to the individual or the church or ministry?" Sometimes I've observed giving of gifts as a way to "buy off" criticism.

Continuing Education and Sabbaticals. Two current "halo concepts" need to be evaluated. Most continuing education events and Sabbaticals are glorified vacations and make no significant change within the individuals. In fact, often a consuming desire for some is a clear indication of anticipated or desired job changes.

Every staff job must build into its week-by-week effort additional education and skill training. The best training events point to expected performance where the staff member will face productive criticism. We must find ways to help each other to do a better job.

Work Hard - Play Hard is an essential ingredient of team building. Whenever one member or a cluster of the team withdraws from common group "Play" then I begin to look for anticipated tension areas. Everyone needs periods of aloneness, but teams need opportunity for creative relaxation and fun.

Planned evaluation is essential. The employing institution has to develop an objective basis for evaluating performance. The Conference Minister must again and again ask how can the team member grow professionally and in responsibility. Each year a session needs to focus upon "what difference did I make?" This evaluation results from a period of goal projection at the beginning of the year. Again, a familiar third party outsider can be a tremendous evaluation help.

Termination - Firing - seems to be the avoided necessity within most voluntary associations. The fact remains not everyone can or should work on a creative leadership team. Some do not want to work as hard as the tasks demand. Some are just incompetent - others belong in other jobs. Whatever the reason, if the facts call for termination, the Conference Minister must act. To put off such a responsibility helps not the team nor the individual involved. There is no sin involved in being fired. One needs to face hard facts and if it means termination then you cannot avoid it and the sooner it's accomplished the better.

SUMMARY

Team building of professionals is an ongoing, never ending process. Status should never be gained from longevity, but only from professional competency. Because a team member might be present longer than the others could be a sign of perceived incompetency (no one wants him). Professional individuals, free to risk, are not afraid of change. Job mobility is often an asset for a learning, competent person brings to a team a variety of experiences (successes and failures) that will help the new and emerging team gestalt. It's not how long a member has been on the team; it's what difference has his presence made.

The Conference Team is not an end in itself. Its task is not to feel so good about each other that it never gets on with its primary task of assisting the Community of Faith to be faithful. Occasionally I've observed some Conference Staffs - or National Staffs - or Seminary Faculties who so enjoy the stimulation of being together that an outsider seeking help feels like an intruder.

**Images
Containing Futures**

Sociality

Sociality is what we feebly refer to when we say "community"
We are born into an intersubjectivity which was going on long before
we came along. We are immersed in it all around . . . we swim **inside**
the ocean.
>This immersion is our fortune . . . a Form of the human and God
>which sustains us. Sometimes it is our disaster.

1

Sociality is living covenant . . . created by
interiorizing each other's inner-personal region
>(and knowing that we have)

taking account of each other's interiority and intent
>as we feel, think, act.

2

When we say "sociality," we are not referring to a surface socializing. Nor a mere imprinting of persons with the social scene.
>In sociality, we have some strong respect for the person(s) we have interiorized. The other strikes us as rightly (but not perfectly) human
>>with sociality we make ourselves manifest to each other somewhat honestly. We would not speak with a forked tongue, delight in being phony, use the other while pretending the opposite.

>There is **intimacy** of interiority. Enough of each other's inner world and attempt to turn earth into meaningful world has been interiorized to bring about a **society** of interiority.

We so dwell in each other (and in something together) that the idea-power, inventing-worlds power, love power of each is available to the other for what is being faced or done; cf. Luther's "saved by grace")
>Together we are creative of more than either alone would ever have brought about.

Sociality is more than a mutuality-in-pleasure. Interiorizing and culturing and taking account of each other matures thru a costly teaming up together against a tough enterprise. Thru costly struggle which reveals where each other's conscience is. Until we have gone thru participating in another's redemption from dark moments (and they in one of our struggles toward new integrity) how can we know that sociality exists? And at what depth and power?
>By gifts of ourselves to the sociality, the sociality is created and purified.

So sociality implies a certain duration. A "dwelling in" suggests some settled and staying power . . . not transitory fragility. We care about what happens to the other, and about what happens to our withness.
>However when we say "withness" and "dwelling in" we do not

mean that we disappear in them, nor they in us. We do not devour each other. Dialogue continues. The I of each remains at the same time there is treasured covenant of livingness.

3

Sociality is not just something whelmed upon me by the fact that I am immersed in the social scene. I have something to do with the state and content of myself as sociality.

I have given these people residence in my heart. They are not merely memories to be retrieved, objects to be coped with . . . but an inner population with which to invent and discriminate.

I have brought this inner population together into what could be called a Beloved Community or a Generalized Other. They hold conversation together with each other when I am in important decision. Together they cumulate (or lose) power as life goes on.

I have brought them together in an order of nearness and intensity. Within my most encompassing sociality must be concentric circles which include "fellow citizens." And most active enemies.

I have cohered human being treasure in a way never before functional together. Unique humanness becomes a From of humankind.

4

Sociality is more than merely liking each other . . . or knowing how the other feels.

Sociality involves common Significant Symbols. In fact a **structure of symbols** which awaken and pull power out of us to bring off an enterprise together.

Sociality may begin with interiorizing and intimacy, but it must become a **culture** — a **system** of meanings and symbols. Memory clusters, potent words, anticipatory resoluteness, persons admired and hated, mythhistory of Our People, song and poetry and anecdotes, television shows talked over, etc.

We cannot **live** the events of our life nor of a sociality apart from dwelling in some system of conceptualizing and valuing and speaking . . . that is larger than ourselves and more insightful.

5

Sociality is most of what we should mean when we say "love." Much of what we could mean when we say "trust" . . . "grace" . . . "human fulfillment." When we say "congregation."

In sociality, there is a religiousness that is substantial, delightful. The human song becomes a symphony.

**Images
Containing Futures**

II

Membranes of Meaning

I. MEMBRANES OF MEANING

By its very nature. a meaning coalesces into a membrane of mind. Lewis Thomas, in "The Lives of a Cell" makes these points about the functions of membranes in the life of every organism —

> In all forms of life on earth. you have to be able to catch energy and hold it ... storing precisely the needed amount. releasing it in relevant measure.
> Membranes enable us to do this.
> To stay alive. you have to be able to hold out against equilibrium ... else your energies flow out and down to the lowest level of surrounding environment (both in amount and quality). Else over time dull sameness comes about in all that is within. Momentum and focus and fragrance and voice dissipate.
> Membranes enable us to bank against entropy. To cumulate and intensify. Without membranes. we could not structure ourselves as a wholeness. As internal cosmos. As a psychic field.

You transact all this business of being human thru the forming and functioning of **membranes of meaning**.

2

> A mind needs "a set of symbols. rituals. paradigms, narratives, and assertions which unite the conscious and unconscious, the secular and the sacred ... and serve to orient and inform. explain and articulate human existence."   (James Cochrane article)

Who's for a ministry of membranes of meaning?

II. MEANING IS TO BE WITH SOMETHING

A person has to see his life **along with** *something.*
> *We can't even see ourselves unless we are in contrast to, or connected with, some background.*

An absolutely 'free-floating I' loses meaning.
To the degree we keep gaining roots in an ecology of spirit and membership in a net of life, meaning fills our consciousness and births meaningful world. **we are meaningful.**

2

To be excellently human, we have to **be with** a Thou ... a Presence we would not take over or violate, but be toward it a tender respectiveness.
Sensing that, to them, we too are a Thou, sensing 'I am an **I-Thou**, and therefore sensing **"I AM"**

3

Something enduringly **means** (and so do we) ... when we can place it within some **scheme of things**, within some field of workings.
We must dwell in some home place. Sense that we are acting **from within**. A people that is moving their time and destiny. And we are understandingly participating in its momentum.
Life has meaning to the degree we know that we **stand in** the depths of life's working.

III. MEANING IS TO SEE-FEEL A DEVELOPMENT

Something means to us when it is **becoming** ... emerging ... birthing ... developing ... journeying ... flaring into crystalline beauty.
We experience ourselves as **meaningful life** when we are a fullness rushing into significant form.
When we are all put together in fresh design that steps all our consciousness up to the speed of light.
When we and our world are no longer diffuse, but a work of art. For we have put together a **life** world ... with our energies mobilized inside it. When we are no longer on dead center.
Meaning comes from being Forming Form. From being generative, procreative. ... in the mode of God creating a universe for the first time. We are not merely a survival, but a creativeness.
The creative play of mind upon mind is consummation of the human.

IV. MEANING IS THE INNER-PERSONAL
ALIVED OR DEADENED

1

A person is an identity ... something he dependably is over a period of time that gives his Inner-Personal region distinction and a center.
Only an identity can live by meanings. Can birth meanings.
With meanings and identity we are an Inner-Personal that experiences, thinks, organizes, stretches into futures that glow with possibility.
Something means when we experience "My Inner-Personal center is **alived** (or being deadened), freshly **membered** (or disjointed and made alone), **developmentally leaps** (or begins to disappear).

With an identity and membranes of meaning we can discriminate, shape up, treasure, what we are. Richness cumulates. Appreciation prevails over disaster.

A **thing** *does not experience meaning. Nor exist by meanings. A person ... an interiority and an intersubjectivity ... does. And so can be an integrity that lives as expressive spontaneity.*

2

With meanings I can intelligently (and with the help of others) identify "friend or foe, me and not me" in what is before me. I can **consider** *"shall I fight, run, ignore, submit, create with, this which I am encountering," I can flexibly choose alternate paths to my goal. I can reconsider and not be so compulsive impulse-wise next time."*

V. MEANING IS THE MATING OF TIMES

Meaning is a product of an almost constant trialogue in our mind of three dimensions of time. Future, past, and present are always talking together, opening a proposed meaningful world. Forming the next theme and the next action of the drama which we are ... which is always an offspring, and not a mere duplication of either of the three corners of time.

So fresh meaning is born, yet we are also a duration. Expectancy surges up new energies, and memory gives them courage.

We *can* **mean.**

A Lived Moment Revisited

BY FRANKLIN R. ELLIOTT
Mayflower Congregational Church
Billings, Montana

THE MOMENT

"May I turn the tables on you?"
My ears heard him plainly, but my voice asked, "What?"
His wife had kindled a family candle and placed it carefully beside the figure of a shepherd boy. With other tiny flames it let us see the creche on the communion table.
Below our bowed and candle-lighted faces, six hands clasped each other within our pressing triad.
I had prayed:
"Eternal God,
the candle we have kindled
and placed before the Christmas creche
is in itself a kind of prayer
—a prayer that there may be light if anywhere in our lives is darkness
—a prayer for warmth if anywhere we harbor coldness
—a prayer that this continued burning might voice our hope,
Our deep desire that the love glowing in our hearts may never be extinguished."
The congregation, seated all around us, could not hear our words; for as the organ played, they joined in carol after well-loved carol and waited their family turn to light a creche-side candle, and form a hand-held circle while I said a family prayer.
Immersed in the music, caressed by the candlelight, embraced in our closeness, we were awed by the Presence to whom we prayed.
I heard my voice say "What?"
And I heard him ask again, "May I turn the tables on you? May I say a prayer?"
With my ready assent he spoke to the Presence.
He evoked our memory of their dead and only son.
He petitioned the loving God for the eternal well-being of the boy and of his friend
both lost on the threshold of their manhood.
He thanked God for the ministry of our church to their family.

As I echoed his "Amen", reflective gleams put tiny candles along three pairs of reverent eyelids.

* * * * * *

A contrived and sentimental Christmas Eve?
To be forgotten before the New Year?
No!
A lived moment
to be fixed in memory
to be revisited again and again
to be mined for its depth of meaning.

THE ANATOMIES OF THE MOMENT

The moment was lived.
Alive it was intense simplicity—a whole.
Revisited it is a diverse complexity—an intricate anatomy.*

Anatomy 1
Society in turmoil

The young
calling into question the value systems of their parents, in rebellion against the warfare of their nation.

New music
words of protest
unrelenting beat
New symbols
the motor cycles, the hair, the clothing

The Father
critical of the cycle
advocating a different life-goal
distressed by the symbols
then
one night on the way to work
not some foolhardy escapade
simply on the way to work
an accident
A careless driver on a city street
collision of auto and cycle
The son is dead.
No chance to watch him grow through his struggles into maturity
No way to say "I would rather hear the throbbing music than this empty silence".
No years when sonship fades and friendship brightens
Only this all-consuming grief-work to endure.

* anatomy (noun) 6. a separating or dividing into parts, aspects, or components in order to make a thorough study . — Webster's Third New International Dictionary.

Anatomy 2

The Christian church accessible

In many times and scattered places Christians had gathered
Two millenia of congregation in the healing spirit of the Christ.

A decade before, a group of Christians had covenanted to be a church in this place.
They had picked a site on the city's edge and built a building.
With their own labor they finished it.
A three-rail pasture fence surrounded it.
Reduced to two rails it became a suburban decoration.
But it needed paint.
So the youth group members invited their peers from a neighboring town to a Tom Sawyer weekend.
The son was one of those who came to help to paint the fence.
Years passed.
The family moved to the city.
But they did not move their church affiliation.
Now this tragedy.
Where to turn?
To the church of the Tom Sawyer weekend.
The church was there for them.
Sharing their sorrow.
Working through their grief.
Welcoming them into its membership.

Anatomy 3

A when-we-always time

The creche-side, candlelighted, carol-singing, family-circled, prayerful custom had become a Christmas Eve tradition.
The father and the mother returned each year to watch the family circles enlarge and diminish, to feel the "holy quiet of the hour", and to say to the memory of their son: we have not forgotten you.

Anatomy 4

The trigger of a new tragedy

One of the son's friends - a very helpful friend when the accident had happened - now stricken himself by a wasting disease.
Shriveled in his young manhood from a muscled athlete to a wisp of skin and skeleton whom his tiny mother could once more cradle in her arms.
Frustrated, bitter, alienated.
Sure that belief in a divine providence is a hope with substance.
Finally a reconciliation with the Steadfast Creativity.
Then on Christmas Eve, the end.
Filled with compounded feeling the father and the mother come into the center of the congregation to light a prayerful candle.

Anatomy 5

Invitation to expression

The climate of the congregation invited personal expression.

At each worship service they gather around the communion table.
They look into each others faces.
Wordless communication is exchanged.
Worshippers **are** members one of another.
And in this particular Advent the encouragement to participate was explicit. A process called the Art of Advent had expected members of the congregation to share their own creations.
A member of the diaconate had said these words in the church newsletter:
When a stir comes in a soul, it needs expression,
Sometimes it becomes a song, a whistle, sometimes a hug.
At Advent the feeling comes anew each year -
with gratitude and praise, quietly, whispering, nudgingly, restlessly.
If ignored it is like a waif at the door -
this time not wanting **in** but **out.**
I invite you to respond to the quiet creativity in you and to share your Christmas "gift" out of talents God has given you.
Your gift may be in friendliness; it may be in song, poetry, telling of wonderful Christmases in the past, painting, the art of cooking - perhaps in trying a new creation this season.
Bring these varied talents with you to the Church this Advent. *

The congregation had responded.
New poets had emerged.
Experienced writers shared their work.
Around the sanctuary paintings stood on easels.
Memories of music offered in this spirit lingered in the atmosphere.
And the burdened tree bore childhood's creativity.

* * * * * *

With this encouragement
breathing this climate
having come to this palce
moved by new sorrow
he said a prayer.

We gripped his hands.
He bowed his head
and spoke from the center of his being
to the Presence who was there at his center
and in our midst.

INSIGHTS FROM THE MOMENT

Searching for the meanings in this Christmas moment went on at the same time as the preparations for the Maundy Thursday service. Out of

* Bette von Hess in *The Log* for November 17, 1976

this circumstance arose an idea which may have been obvious to others all along.

The communion service is a lived moment revisited.

Overlaid as it is with tradition, still the incident happened. Once in an upper room Jesus broke some matzos and shared some wine in a way which endured in memory and ritual.

The enduring quality of that moment was not in the bread or in the wine. It was in all the influences which made the moment possible — and in their focusing. It was in the events it illumined in retrospect for the disciples. And it is revisited in the meanings which are mined from its depths each time the ceremony is celebrated.

The Lord's Supper is a lived moment with anatomies and insights.

Having reached that conclusion I began to wonder whether all Christian ceremonies are "lived moments revisited", and I began to draw some distinctions.

Communion is a lived moment revisited. Holy Week is. So are the Nativity Celebrations. Funerals are lived moments themselves. So are baptisms and weddings.

Heritage out of the history and personal experience of the present are in both. In a lived moment personal exigencies are the focal point. They influence the content and set the time. Revisited the focus shifts to the heritage. It dominates the content and the scheduling.

Last Christmas Eve a lived moment revisited turned into a lived moment itself.

* * * * * *

This father brought his whole self to the sanctuary.

He brought his physical body — a body with eyes that fill with tears, a body with nerves that feel the sorrow aching inside the angle of the jaw bones, that note the weight of grief upon the rib cage — a body with brain and voice that shape the paragraphs of prayer.

He brought his internal congregation of relationships. He came inhabited by the son, the wife, the friends, the associates, the relatives, the ancestors.

He carried with him the experiences life had given him and the choices he had made in response. When the first tragedy happened, the father had many options. He chose to grow through the experience — to open himself to unfamiliar viewpoints, to become an energy source for others, to search for meanings in the stimulating and the destructive, the pleasant and the aggravating, the loving and the troublesome.

His spirit — the concreteness of this wholeness — was present, open to the mysteries of faith, willing to risk him with his wife, with me, with the climate of the congregation, with the presence of God.

And he did turn the tables. He ministered to me.

Christian ceremonies which involve the worshippers in authentic participation gather into themselves the lived moments of our existence and become openings into mutual ministry.

Storifying by the Listener As A clue to Preaching

(A conversation with Paul Davis, pastor First Congregational Church, Webster Groves, Mo.)

Davis: I am interested in the power of story to animate and serve the cause of God in Christ in the areas of worship and religious education and pastoral care.

My interest began on an Advent Sunday morning several years ago. In worship the church was that day celebrating the coming incarnation of God in Christ, and scripturally, the service based itself in Matt. 1:23. "And his name shall be called Emmanuel" (God with us)." Early in the service, this scripture was read. In the prayers these phrases were included. Then in the sermon I told this story: "I remember being in Woolworth's as a six year old boy with my father, and it was Christmas and Santa Claus was there. And Santa Claus was either underpaid or angry, or just had a fight with his wife, for as I met him that day I holding my father's hand, Santa Claus, looking down said to me "Paul, you have been a bad boy this year." And I, in my self-righteousness and boyhood fear, said back to Santa Claus, "but it must be another boy named Paul, perhaps someone who lives in my neighborhood and who looks somewhat like me." And he said, sternly, "no, Paul, no you have been a bad boy." And I felt my insides shrivel and I turned away sweaty-palmed with all the inherited guilt of the race since Adam coming home to haunt me. And my father, being my father, would have hit Sant Claus if I hadn't been there and if it hadn't been Christmas. Instead, he turned and walked me out past the candy counter to the street again, and I will always remember my father holding my hand firmly as we walked, and I held his. At the moment I didn't have Santa Claus but I had my father. My father I was sure of, and I knew he understood me and approved and cared. "God with us. Immanuel."

Snyder: Paul, I'd like to develop with you the original experience, and then come later to your experience in preaching in the church service.

Is it correct to say that there were two strands in your boyhood experience? One was a strand of disaster: "Paul, you have been a bad boy all year." And along with that was another strand, "But my father is with me." Can you recall how those two strands battled within you at the time?

Davis: Yes, I remember looking up into the face of that man and being just incredulous. Because, you know, I'd kept the law, and it had to be a mistake. Because I couldn't be bad. I sensed that either he was drunk . . . or probably angry. And I felt just devastated.

At that point I remember the firmness of Dad's hand holding me. We didn't say anything. I remember feeling that my Dad was kind of puzzled, and that my Dad would have hit him under different circumstances. I remember he wheeled me around and we walked out past the caramel counter where I used to like to stop. We just went clear right on out. I knew that he was angry and determined. Because he normally would have stopped and compensated with candy, but we went clear out into the open air. And I had the illusion in fantasy that he might have walked back to settle accounts with Santa Claus later, but I'm not sure.

Yes, I remember very intensely that man in a white beard looking down into me. I just feel the sweaty palm, the all-shriveled-up feeling inside me, myself unable to cope with this giant of a man who at that moment had so got me down. And then my father firmly walking with me, not over me.

Snyder: In any situation that happens there's always more than one strand of feeling going on. So often we talk about just the one strand. But you have lifted up both strands which I think makes for a much more important experience.

Davis: A friend with whom I have shared this anecdote feels it is important that we walked past the candy counter — candy representing what the culture does at Christmas, Santa representing what the culture does at Christmas. We walked out under the stars.

Snyder: Your father and you didn't stop at the candy counter, to try to assuage what had happened and the hurt you had by a palliative of candy, but you walked out into the stars. You were getting out of the factual situation, into another kind of world. A world not composed by this Santa Claus.

Davis: Santa Claus was stuffed back into the back of that Woolworth's and I almost felt my father was just instinctively getting us clear out of that mind-set into another. I'm not sure Dad thought about all this; we never talked about it. He never mentioned it again. He was all action.

Snyder: "We don't have to live in this hell."

Davis: Yes

Snyder: He was not going to have his boy made captive to that kind of world.

The **major** impression that you reported, however, was not so much the visual memory as the memory of your dad's hand firmly hold of yours.

Davis: Yes, I remember my sweaty palm, my shriveling insides before Santa. And then the warmth and firmness of just being walked right on out. Quietly, but firmly. In hand, companions.

Snyder: That's become a symbol for you almost all your life.

Davis: Well, yes. In many ways theologically in that I think the subtlety of it has become important for me. I'm not a triumphalist theologically at all and would be more attuned to a quiet companionship which doesn't have to bespeak itself much. That just passes up some things like candy counters. Rather than directly taking them on in every case and debating.

Snyder: Let's be sure what you're saying here. Your dad didn't necessarily stop in a situation like that and say, "Now Paul, you're feeling very badly about this guy and let's do a little bit of psychological therapy here." There was something else that you believe was the crucial thing that he did.

Davis: "Purity of heart to will one thing," Roy Larson said last night . . . I thought of this incident as he said that, because there was a willing in a singular sort of a fashion by my father. A nonverbal one which simply moved into the situation very quietly but with determination, with intention and did something with it that was noble. No analysis. No equivocation. And so the Immanuel, God with us scripture really struck me as I was struggling preparing that Advent sermon.

Snyder: Let's go with the Advent sermon, then. You were working on the phrase "God with us," and this memory came up?

Davis: Yes, I was working also with Easter proposition "Lo I am with you always to the close of the age". . . bringing that in touch with Christmas. And I tried to think of some experience where the meaning was alive. And all of a sudden that sense of being hand and hand going out past the candy counter came to mind.

Snyder: In thinking about contemporary celebration, I've come to nominate that little preposition "**with**" as one of the most important theological words we can understand and use. Sometimes we're doing the most important depth theologizing when we are off the official big language.

Let's come to your memories of preaching the sermon.

Davis: After the Scripture, and some brief development of it, I moved into that story. I was right in the middle of it, telling it just as I have here . . . when I became suddenly aware of an atmosphere about the congregation that was a little scary. The attention was so real, they were so enraptured in it. And I thought "what are we into here?" So much so that I almost lost my concentration and had a little trouble finishing the story. But I did. After the service I went back and talked to some people about "what was going on there this morning?"

It suddenly occurred to me that we had touched some kind of a flow of power that I had not previously dealt with very often in preaching. The involvement of many in the congregation startled me. They seemed to be launched on waves of their own fantasy. Their faces pleased and soaring. It was the same lifted move of collected revery that I was to sense later on many, many other Sunday mornings, as the congregation worshipped and I paid attention to the power of story in the gathered worship experience. I began to notice both when I preached and when some of the other people on the staff preached, that there was a kind of a soaring, dreaming, involvement and revery that was going on. I think what happens is that people really are listening to this story, but they're also fantasizing into their own stories.

Snyder: What do you mean fantasizing? That word really bothers me.

Davis: Well, by fantasizing, I mean they're imagining their way into their own stories.

Snyder: They're reliving their own stories.

Davis: They're reliving their own stories, right.

Snyder: They're not only re-living their own stories, they're re-meaning their own stories? For me "fantasy" is a thin word for what is going on.

I'd like to say they're re-imagining and newly living their stories, while living with you the sudden depth of your experience. So there's a double level going on. Maybe a triple level if they're taking in also the scriptural.

Davis: There's the scriptural story, their story, and the story being told to them. And they're not only listening in a cognitive way to what is being said, they're launched off into circles.

Snyder: You have there then a concept of what could go on in really productive preaching. And you have energies in motion about this. For the concept has inside it the fires of a situation that occurred to you personally.

Davis: In a sermon by another friend the same thing happened about six months later, and I suddenly became aware of this intense involvement again, and yet not a hard rectangular involvement. It had a dreaming, soaring quality. And as I watched people and later checked it out with many, they were both into the story of his childhood that he was telling plus into similar stories in their childhoods ... a kind of stories circling one over the other in such a way that they were seeing back over the two or three levels at once.

Snyder: Would it be going too far to say that they were not just reliving the stories, but that the playing back and forth that you're speaking of was finally a **process of creating a new kind of a world that they felt they lived in?**

Davis: I would say yes to that. Much of my thesis was an effort to get at that way in which we storify the world, create storied existence. Life as story.

Snyder: So that when we're talking about life as story, we're also talking about the way that every human consciousness is always creating a world to live and a world to live in. And unless our listeners are about re-meaning and re-creating these images of world they are living, they're not at much religious depth.

Davis: You say that until they do that ...

Snyder: Yes.

Davis: Yes I've come to feel that. It has something to do with imagination. That's the way I've been moving more and more — learning to re-image the world and yourself with the power of a vivid picture, and connecting that with vividness in gospel and in the history of the church.

Snyder: To keep deepening this point ... you're developing a theory of preaching those energies and design have originations back in this vivid boyhood experience. If you had not begun with such primoridal experience — first of being assaulted by monstrous evil that made unfair judgments upon you, not even knowing anything about you, and secondly the experience memory of the firm actuality of your father's hand holding yours, symbolizing to you the whole relationship you were sure about — your present power in preaching would not be. To those two primordials, we should add a third experience — your sensing the experiencing of your people listening. And your trust to find out "what's going on here?"

Davis: I remember talking to a friend of mine who had lost their daughter, and he said to me one time that in listening to people speak of the death of a child, that within a few minutes he can pretty well tell whether they've really been there. Because of what one might call the density of description. A story-telling begins to either trail off into the theoretical description, or it moves on into density of involvement. In the words used and the tone of voice.

Snyder: Will you expound that word "density" for us?

Davis: My father's hand in mine in his would be density, whereas to analyze that scene very much ... or had Dad sat down and said "well, this terrible thing has happened. Let's talk it over. That would move off to a more fragile, abstracted level." Density would be involvement in the moment and in the touch of the moment.

Snyder: Every good word gets trivialized after a while, and that can happen to what you've gotten hold of. And if all over the country ministers start saying that story-telling is the secret of preaching — and they don't understand something of what is meant by that as you understand it — then we're just going to have another gimmick that's going to run its day, and within a year from now, everyone will be looking for another gimmick. Phenomenologizing as I understand it is always trying to get back down to the level of the fundamental process, and not just let people take the surface off the word or an idea ...

Davis: Yes, Ross, I guess I'd like to say that as I think of story-telling and storifying as a form of religion, it's not just telling stories. A few of those may help, but it's trying to help a mood happen which can probably be animated here and there by a good graphic phrase. But what I'm after is more than telling a story. What I'm after doesn't really happen if they stay with my story. **The task is to get them into their story.** Sometimes that happens through some good graphic gripping phrases that move them into their density.

For example, I've come to feel that leading worship is really not what I thought it was when I came out of seminary, and for about the first 10 years. It was a very ego-centered concept, trying to hold people's attention, and cause something cognitive to take place, on a **linear plane** all the way through. That's very hard work, and it's kind of anti-productive. Now I have come to feel that preaching and worship is a series of departures and returns for the person in the pew, and for me in the pulpit. My function is to help them launch and return. It's kind of like throwing a frisbee. And if I can just throw it periodically and let them soar on it, it's kind of what the Gregorian chant and its cadence can do. We have become so cognitive and verbal! So storification is that you get into a storified mood which not only helps them get into their background story, their heritage, but also helps them to sense the storification of the present moment when we're worshipping, and their present hour in their lives.

Snyder: I'm still struggling to know how to regard the word "cognitive". Because my impressions are that finally it was a real cognitive grasp of the experience that you originally had which has made you powerfully free to bring off the kind of preaching you are now capable of. It's this combination of elemental experience with cognitive grasp that gives density (which rightly for you is a fundamental value). "Cognitive" is at least half of what you are about. I would hope that "cognitive" doesn't confine us to abstract verbalisms which have no personal human content, but are deposits from reading somebody else's book. I don't want "cognitive" to get into bad repute. Maybe the point is for what purposes we do the cognitive. So how do you use "Cognitive?"

Davis: Would you buy "cerebral?"

Snyder: What would people be without cerebral functioning? That's the uniting, the integrating, that puts it all together in some kind of form, and with larger connections. If all you have is guts! Who wants to live with people who live as a crocodile mind? The terrorists and the torturers are doing that already.

Davis: And I'm certainly not at the point in my own philosophy.

Snyder: I'm concerned that "cognitive" and "cerebral" become smear words, and people plan themselves as distortions of the human.

Davis: I guess I'm trying to say that certainly we're talking about a mental process including whole body process. But that it all comes alive probably more to graphic image which is reacting to a conceptual frame or vice versa, than it does in extended linear (I almost said cognitive, but I I want to say "abstractive material"). I'd rather wrap tough cognitive in the sense of theological, philosophical cognitive, in a very direct way with solid scene and graphic image and let those two work in polarity. I'd rather do that than speak for very long in a Sunday morning church situation in what we will then call an abstractive, argumentative, defining fashion.

Snyder: When are you going to write the book?

A Pastoral Perspective on Marriage and Family Counseling

BY JOHN PATTON
Executive Director,
Georgia Association for Pastorial Care

I am a pastoral counselor who spends the majority of his clinical time in marriage and family counseling. I do this for two reasons: (1) because the majority of referrals which come to me as a pastoral counselor involve a presenting problem of marriage or family pain; and (2) because working with couples and families is more fun. I assure you that the two reasons are in some way related.

My experience as a patient involves both individual and couple's psychotherapy. My family, which includes my wife, three teen-agers and a ten year old, has not yet been a patient together. My training in counseling and psychotherapy has been at one time or another client-centered, psychoanalytically-oriented and experiential. My training in theology and ministry has been at a denominational school of theology (Emory University) and an ecumenical graduate school of religion (The University of Chicago).

I believe that the practice of marriage and family counseling is and ought to be affected significantly by assumptions and beliefs about the nature of marriage and the family derived from the Judeo-Christian tradition and from counseling practice understood as a dimension of ministry. I would like to identify some of those assumptions and beliefs and then suggest their implications for practice. First, the nature of marriage and the family.

To move toward the assumptions which inform my practice, I would like to point to two somewhat contradictory Biblical texts, one from the Old Testament and one from the New. "It is not good that the man should be alone;" (Gen. 2:18) and "For in the resurrection they neither marry nor are given in marriage." (Matt. 22:30) One suggests the importance of intimate relationship; the other, its temporality. Leaving aside questions of the authority of these texts, particularly when wrenched from their contexts, I would argue that they suggest a Christian view of marriage which insists upon both the development of individual personhood and the growth which is possible only in an intimate relationship of commitment and continuity.

In both Old and New Testaments, commitment and continuity of relationship are seen not so much as referent to marriage but to be a part of the very nature of God. In spite of human inconsistency and unfaithfulness, God gives himself in a binding, future-oriented involvement with a particular people. The theme of divine promise, of fulfillment and meaning is a central message of the Bible. Human response involves faith in this promise in spite of massive evidence of meaninglessness and temporality. Human relationships, then, are to be undertaken with a spirit similar to that of God's covenant with persons in Christ. Like that covenant they involve a commitment to affirm another in spite of his or her sin, and a willingness to struggle together toward a future that is ultimately in God's hands.

This kind of personal commitment involves a willingness to allow the committed relationship to be viewed as a part of God's larger history with his people, to be the type of relationship which is defined by that larger context, to grow and develop in new and unexpected ways and to be judged ultimately by God; it involves a willingness to celebrate the given commitment as occasion for living fully in the covenant he has given.

A development or extension of the meaning of our first test, then, in the light of this understanding of commitment, would be, "It is good for men and women to be committed to another person, for in such a relationship he or she not only relieves loneliness, but partially exemplifies or illustrates God's commitment to persons and their ultimate value." A development of the second text would be, "Although a committed human relationship reveals something of the character of God, no relationship is permanent, and one which becomes an end in itself obscures the freedom and destiny of the person as revealed by the symbol of resurrection, i.e. ultimately related through Christ to God alone." Both individual personhood, viewed as having eternal significance in the light of God's covenant, and the importance of committed relationships is at the heart of the Biblical message.

My assumptions, then, about marriage and the family, in the light of this understanding of commitment and covenant, are that these institutions are important, but not eternal. Marriage and the family grow out of a very practical human problem, loneliness, and should not be romanticized or elevated in importance. They should, rather, be seen as major opportunities for the development of personhood in the light of God's affirmation of us and our commitment to each other. Such relationships should, therefore, be entered into and exited from "discreetly, advisedly, soberly, and in the fear of God," and, perhaps with the assistance of a competent marriage and family counselor. Now, to an understanding of counseling as a dimension of ministry.

The term, "pastoral," is appropriately used as a modifier for "counseling" when the process so described is primarily understood as a ministry of a specific religious community or communion. Whatever techniques are used, the counseling so identified is fundamentally an effort to help persons—in this context, a couple or a family—to discover a sense of personal meaning and destiny and to live more effectively in the light of that meaning. Pastoral counseling involves both a recognition of the reality of sin, understood as alienation from God and from one another, and the possibility of redemption, understood as growth toward wholeness in spite of sin's bondage. Though the nature of the problems presented may be identified as marital or family, e.g., infidelity, sexual frustration, role conflict, etc., marriage and family counseling which is "pastoral" can never be understood primarily as the solving of those specific problems. It is a response to the human situation, a predicament to be lived, not a problem to be solved, which involves the offering of a caring relationship.

Pastoral marriage and family counseling may be understood as a religious process in that it involves the discovering and living of personal meaning in the context of family relationships. Such counseling deals, usually implicitly, with traditional religious questions like, Who am I? What is my place in the world? What must I do to be saved? Although presenting problems are more likely to be expressed, to a specialized minister of pastoral counseling at least, in terms such as, depression or marital conflict rather than religious quest, the pastoral counselor's assumption is that these problems are more likely to be solved if the quest for meaning rather than the specific problem is viewed as primary.

In the light of a specifically Christian religious tradition, counseling that is pastoral can usefully be understood as the discovery or rediscovery of personal meaning, a sense of destiny and purpose, through relational humanness, the norm for which is God's humanness for and with us in

Jesus Christ. God's relation to the world through a person strongly suggests that the clue for development of personal meaning in life rests in the quality of relationships and the character of humanness revealed in that person. Questions about the adequacy of pastoral counseling, therfore, should most often be raised with respect to relational quality and richness of humanity revealed in the counseling process. If the relationship between the counselor and the couple or family with which he or she is working is not powerfully evident, genuine pastoral counseling is not taking place. If the counselor's humanness is not evident and counselees' not respected and sought after, what is going on is not pastoral counseling.

The norm for pastoral counseling, relational humaness, suggests a psychotherapeutic understanding of marriage and family counseling in that it is more often concerned with character change and growth than with problem solving. This emphasis on change and growth is, however, more a part of the religious tradition than the psychological or medical. The methods used for change and the context in which change takes place may not be traditional ecclesiastical ones, but the goal of freedom in relationship is one which the religious community has traditionally sought after.

Now I have given some of my assumptions and beliefs about marriage and the family in the light of my religious tradition and my understanding of pastoral counseling or counseling understood as a dimension of ministry. I shall now try to demonstrate how these views may influence my practice as a marriage and family counselor (although it is clear that the influence works both ways).

First of all, the patient for marriage and family counseling is both the marriage or family unit and each of the individuals involved in that unit. The marriage or family system is significant, but not ultimate. From a pastoral perspective, a therapeutic technique which works only with the system and is not in some way significantly related to the persons involved is ruled out. A pastoral relation to the system is also relationship to the individuals therein.

Second, a pastoral perspective affirms the wisdom of marital choice and assumes that there is a mystery here that can only be partially understood. The marital relationship as Jesus suggests in the Gospels is not ultimate, but it is more serious, and psychologically unconscious than a purely romantic or voluntaristic choice can make it. Marriages are not made in heaven, but there is enough irrational wisdom in that saying to cause pastors and marriage counselors to respect deeply the marital pairing that confronts us. We will not assume that because our rationality allows us to see no good in a marriage that the couple should get an amicable divorce and get some counseling so that they can do better next time. We, rather, should look with awe at the individual and relational growth that is being worked out in the marriage. This is not to say that a pastoral perspective rules out divorce. It does say, however, that the pastoral counselors may appropriately be highly skeptical of their own knowledge of what makes a workable marriage and awed by the potential for growth which is present even in "impossible" situations.

Third, conventional wisdom derived from other relationships does not apply in any simple form to marriage. As veteran couples therapist John Warkentin has said, "All's fair in love and war, and marriage is both." Learning what **is** (discovering one's sin) is more useful than working with what **ought** to be. Intimacy and depth are far more a feeling than a thinking experience. It is not surprising, therefore, that pain and brokeness are normative for marriage and family relationships. It is not possible to learn enough or learn the right things in order to avoid relational pain. Marriage enrichment, then, is appropriately a search for depth rather than avoidance of problems; likewise, marital therapy is not getting rid of what is broken, but working it through. The normal developmental impasses of marriage do not lend themselves to problem solving behavioral approaches, whether they be prayer or psychological conditioning. They are human mysteries to be lived through with the help of a more experienced pilgrim.

Fourth, the move toward divorce can often be understood as a healthy need for distance and freedom which can be found in a marriage rather than apart from it. Human intimacy needs are so great that the pastoral counselors often experience couples to be like the one described in the mildly obscene limerick: "There was a young couple named Kelly; who were found stuck belly to belly; for in their haste; they used library paste; instead of petroleum jelly." Counseling technique requires that couples be pulled apart, and some of their insatiable dependency needs to be met temporarily in the counseling relationship. They can learn through a pastoral relationship to feed emotionally in relationships other than the marriage, so that the marriage relationship can be unique, or at least adult—one which offers more meat than milk.

Fifth, the nuclear family in our mobile society is often cut off from adequate parenting; therefore, marriage and family counseling from a pastoral perspective should be intergenerational, experiential learning. Marriage counseling is two-generational; family counseling, three-generational. The extended intergenerational family of our forebears is necessary for adequate emotional growth. The skilled pastoral counselor functions as a parent or grandparent, and on occasion son or daughter, in order to reduce the demandingness of a nuclear family's alliances and provide an experience of relational humanness. The counselor functions symbolically or transferentially in the various parenting roles relevant for the marital couple in order that they may re-establish their own individual growth processes and learn to say good-bye at all stages of the developmental process are major elements in marriage and family counseling from a pastoral perspective.

Sixth, interpretation in marriage and family counseling from a pastoral perspective draws less upon traditional psychoanalytic insight than upon the religious and philosophical tradition of hermeneutics. Because relationship is primary, much interpretation is directed there, but the major purpose of interpretation is to deliteralize and enrich our conception of life's journey—our growth in commitment and individuality. This view of interpretation agrees with the Jungians and literalism is damnation and with Whitehead that it is more important that a proposition be interesting than that it be true. Persons in families are trapped by their ways of looking at life; therefore, the counselor suggests alternative views and helps them move back and forth between actual event and symbolic interpretation.

Seventh, the method of pastoral counseling is primarily, but not wholly, verbal. A useful guideline lies in the understanding of ministry as involving both word and sacrament. Christian traditions vary as to the relative importance of each, but seem unified in the view that both word and sacrament must be present where a whole ministry is taking place. Words are not adequate without other behavioral or bodily experiencing as well, but bodily or sacramental experiencing without proper interpretation is incomplete.

I have presented some assumptions and beliefs which, I believe, make up a pastoral perspective on marriage and family counseling, and I have suggested some ways in which these views inform my practice. Whether these beliefs make me a better or a worse marriage and family counselor is for my counselees and those who have to hear me talk about what I do to decide. For me, this perspective makes both the doing and the talking about it more fun, more satisfying or more something. Beyond the personal, however, what liabilities or advantages does a pastoral perspective give a marriage and family counselor?

To the extent that this perspective provides a realistic and useful understanding about human personhood and human destiny, I believe it makes an important contribution to marriage and family counseling. Human relationships are too difficult to bother with unless there is some ultimate value in those who anxiously enter them. If there is, then neither problem solving nor marital health is a large enough concept for describing the goal of those relationships. The sense that the commitment and freedom of marriage is a way of discovering more of God's commitment to and covenant with us is a large enough concept. Marriage and family counseling may be a way in which persons discover that truth more clearly than in church.

Obviously, an ordained clergyperson does not hold any monopoly on this perspective. He or she has simply made a more visible commitment to its validity. The clergyperson has agreed to stay bothered with the meaning of a pastoral perspective and continually to look with his or her religious communion at his or her practice to see if it can indeed be understood as ministry. That is a bother, sometimes a rather costly one, but hopefully, one that has value. Both the parochial minister and the specialized pastoral counselor make use of this perspective and function as marriage and family counselors. The difference here is that the specialist has or should have more freedom and skill to work with the counseling relationships without the complication of other social or parochial relationships.

With respect to other professionals in the marriage and counseling field, I believe that theological training for the general practice of ministry provides as good a basic training for marriage and family counseling as does medicine, psychology, social work, or education. Moreover, given similar adequate training in marriage and family counseling, supervision in the use of one's person in helping relationships, etc., I believe that continued commitment to and study of the religious-theological perspective can facilitate development in one's professional practice at least as well as continued study in psychological theories and techniques.

The Cry of the Heart for Home

BY TRUMAN A. MORRISON
Edgewood United Church, East Lansing, Michigan

Through the years of my ministry in the parish church, many personal convictions have developed and deepened, but none of them with greater certitude than the belief that a primordial drive of the human spirit is to find one's way to life in community of the kind to which the New Testament witnesses, community which has the character of what the mind and heart define as "home"!

I am speaking of "home" in the essential sense of the image of freedom and mutuality we carry in our minds and hearts and of which actual homes usually give us only a tantalizing glimpse. I am speaking of an environment where one may experience the creative interdependence of being and belonging; where personal depths of feeling and thought may be freely explored and expressed in a context of moral seriousness and also of acceptance and forgiveness; an environment where threatening experiences associated with human loneliness, finitude and meaninglessness are treated with the utmost seriousness, but where other modes of being come into view—the kind we associate with personal creativity and freedom, with interpersonal revelation and clarification.

In such a milieu, the "good-news" of an ultimate love and goodness revealed in Jesus Christ takes on a profound existential meaning. I am speaking of the kind of creative community for which the image of home and family are symbols—an image which propels us with the force of something infinitely precious we have previously experienced. And although such quality of life is presently obscured in our existence, we sense that it represents the human authenticity for which we are intended!

I am here referring us to what Ross Snyder would call a "conceptualized primordial," one which I would term, "the cry of the heart for home"! And I would suggest that the lure and power of many of the major images and symbolical stories of the Old and New Testaments are related to this human cry. I am thinking for example, of the mytho-poetic account of the Garden of Eden and the Fall. Adam is the symbol of every human being's awareness that he or she has fallen away from an intended wholeness and completeness. One cannot return in innocence to such a state of congruence, any more than one can simply accommodate one's self to the ambiguous present; a person must go forward into the future driven by the dreams of home!

Jesus' story of the Prodigal Son is endlessly suggestive in this regard, as it deals symbolically with the issues of freeedom and mutuality, alienation and reconciliation, and a Transcendent Love to which we ultimately "come home"! We would have no sense of separation from the Transcendent or from other human beings if we did not also have an underlying sense of relatedness and intended unity with these larger realities. Our very awareness of our existential estrangement witnesses in the indirect way to the truth of our essential relatedness to life.

We are restless in our estrangement because love is the law of life and of our own deepest being. Here the term "love" refers to ever so much more than emotion; it designates a power which works within us all as a hunger for wholeness and a drive to give meaning and pattern to our world, as well as integrity to our lives—impelling us to seek ever higher forms of truth, beauty and goodness. In Christian terms such love is "of God" and of the deepest ground of our being.

All such biblical imagery as that of Eden and the Fall or Jesus' story of the Prodigal resonates with the inner meaning of one's pilgrimage in life, namely, that each of us seeks to make of the world around us a home! We are driven and lured by a desire to overcome in ourselves and in the world the things which deny and inhibit the love, the security of soul, the sense of identity and personal dignity that we connect in our minds with the idea of home and family! Arthur Miller once commented on the world's great dramas — **Hamlet, King Lear, Oedipus** — by saying that all of them "examine the concept of the loss and deprivation of a once existing state of bliss unjustly shattered, a state of equilibrium which the hero is attempting to recreate with new, latter-day life materials. It is as though both dramatist and audience believe they once had an identity, a being, somewhere in the past which in the present has lost its completeness ... The central force making for pathos in these large and thrusting plays is the paradox which time bequeaths to us all: we cannot go home again, and the world we live in is an alien place."

The above observation by a percipient playwright reveals an understanding that our deepest search in life is for authentic community, for the true home of the human spirit. Not merely for the lost family or parents of our youth but for what Thomas Wolfe called, "the image of a strength and wisdom external to our need and superior to our hunger, to which the belief and power of one's own life can be united."

You and I recognize this as an expression of need for what the theologian calls "God" and "the people of God" — a community "grasped and formed by an ultimate concern." In James Luther Adams' words, "God is the inescapable, commanding reality that sustains and transforms all meaningful existence," a "reality that is dependable and in which we may place our confidence"; a "reality that has within it the seeds of becoming, even in the face of tragedy and death." Thus the theologian goes on to affirm that "a sustaining meaning is discernable and commanding in the here and now. Every blade of grass, every work of art, every scientific endeavor, every striving for righteousness bears witness to this meaning. Indeed, every frustration or perversion of truth, beauty or goodness also bears this witness, as the shadow points round to the sun."

Let us go another step and observe that whereas the primordial drive of the human spirit toward the kind of community that is symbolized by home is perennially present in human life, it is particularly apparent in the lives of people today. We live in a time when millions of folk seek to move beyond "the barren universe of impersonal facts" which science reports and technology creates — to find the larger universe which resonates with the human presence and in which we experience as humans our intended reciprocity with each other, with the world of nature and with the ultimate Source of life's creativity and meaning that we call, "God".

The contemporary environment is, indeed, so barren and bereft of human resonance that we have grown accustomed to the works of artists, dramatists and novelists — interpreters of the spirit of the times — as being dark and dour: a Giacometti with his elongated sculptured figures, durable but pervaded by a surrounding void; a Jean Paul Sartre with his nihilistic characters professing a total lack of common human meaning and absolutizing their separateness and strangeness.

It is not fair to speak of all such sensitive spirits in these terms. For the case is different with an insightful interpreter of the times like the brilliant novelist who writes from this very campus, Saul Bellow. In his latest work, **Humboldt's Gift** Bellow is true to his awareness of the bewildering ambiguities and contradictions of life but in, through and beyond these, he apprehends the larger spiritual reality that interfuses and transcends our world of space and time. Like Whitehead, the philosopher, he is responsive to the vision of that which is "beyond, behind and within the passing flux of immediate things". This is the religious vision "without which human life is a flash of occasional enjoyments lighting up a mass of pain and misery, a bagatelle of transient experience." And, like another contemporary, Werner Heisenberg, the great physicist, Bellow is enamored not only with the human soul but with what one's soul intimates of other "truth that dwells in the deeps" — behind "the ordering structures of this world, a consciousness, a central order (an inner core of being) which can be reached as one would reach the soul of a human being . . ."

It is precisely this "feeling for the infinite," as Carl Jung called it, which has been lost by millions of folk — leading us, as Jung said, to "lay stress on false possessions" and to have "less sensitivity for what is essential." A society which has exalted the "cult of logistics and expediency" and allowed "adoration of the new Baal, Society" to eclipse its consciousness of the cosmos, has, in Arthur Koestler's words, "severed its relations with the infinite, isolated itself from the universe, or, if you like, from God." Such spiritual deprivation often leads people to ersatz faiths; like the millions who turn to astrology today to find a personal relationship to the larger universe.

A true perception of the common plight today will reveal, I believe, that in the calculative, if not the exploitative, mode with which people in Western societies have largely addressed their world, we have made the achievement of community virtually impossible. We are now having to learn again how to approach the world "dialogically," as Martin Buber would say, or, in Martin Heidegger's terms, how to assume again an attitude of "glassenheit" or true openness to the Voice of Being.

It has become increasingly clear that without the continually renewed and deepened experience of reciprocity in the inner-human world, our sense of ultimate reality and of the larger universe becomes dreadfully impersonal! Then our experience of God is to be expressed largely in terms of "God as void or enemy" and not as "companion or friend" — to use the terms of Whitehead.

Work within a university church for twenty years has brought me increasingly to the conviction that for most human beings, there is an inextricable linkage between an experienced love in human community and a vitalizing experience of the love of God! Jesus, in effect, made this linkage in the two love commandments. And John asks bluntly in his epistle, "If we do not love our brothers and sisters whom we have seen, how can we love God whom we have not seen?" Paul's organismic concept of the church as the Body of Christ is of a piece with this understanding of the way in which human beings, genuinely present to one another, form a milieu for the working of the divine power that was in Jesus Christ.

In our own day, Ross Snyder has contributed immeasurably to an understanding of how such corporateness comes into being; in his words, a "culture of remembered experiences, meanings, valuings, ideas, significant symbols held together by religious vision"; a community whose culture "indwells each member and something of each indwells the enveloping community"; a people "which keeps putting together a story" which is its own, reflecting "a style of religious consciousness," and yet related to the One Great Story; a "people grasped by the numinous presence, by an Otherness transcendent to its life together."

It is clear from Paul's letters to the early churches that as he writes of the Body of Christ, he is speaking of the life of an actual congregation and not of some ideal or invisible reality; a congregation with flaws and limitations but in which there is real participation in the life of the Spirit, a life defined essentially by love! This love is an "earnest" or foretaste of the larger life to come, for which "the creation wait with eager longing"; this love is also an immediate response to the primordial yearning of the human heart. We are here confronting an ontological reality, in that "there is nothing deeper or more fundamental to one's being than this, that one is made in and for the love of God."

In keeping with the rest of the Old and New Testament, Paul's letters stress this concept of corporateness, an understanding of God's saving work as it takes place within the life of a community, a people of God. This is, indeed, the thread that binds together the diverse elements of the Bible, the history of a people in which "salvation" is understood as a healing or making whole of the human and the divine — a saving reality which is both corporate and cosmic! In the inspired words of Leslie Newbigin, "The new humanity in Christ . . . into which we would fain grow up is a corporate humanity . . . The restoration of the broken harmony, between all human beings and between human beings and God, between humanity and nature . . . must be communicated in and by the actual development of a community which embodies — if only in foretaste — the restored harmony (of creation) of which it speaks."

In the New Testament the emphasis on corporateness leads explicitly into the cosmic! The love which is known in the Body of Christ belongs to the basic and ultimate reality of the universe, to that which abides when all else is dissolved! The saving love is not known in its fullness; "We see through a glass darkly." But is a love in which we may trust and abide. To abide in this love is to abide in God, and the self-giving character of such love impells us into a life of outgoing concern and continuing pilgrimage. A new experience of corporateness and a new relationship to the cosmos speak profoundly to the yearning of the heart for home; but the new reality lures us on toward "the city which hath foundations, whose builder and maker is God."

It is my experience that as the emphasis on corporateness and cosmos takes effect in the life of a congregation, an appreciation deepens for the centrality of the Lord's Supper. The common sharing of the Loaf and the Cup becomes a visible bond of participation in the Body of Christ. Also, the church as a family takes on a new meaning, along with the concept of "the extended family." Such a development can speak to the beleagured state of the nuclear family in American society today and can assist church-related families to join with others in various kinds of family clusters under the aegis of the church. In such a context, responsibilities are shared, mutual problems faced, relationships explored, generational conflicts and commonalities clarified, family and community concerns addressed, new life-styles examined, mutual support provided for more venturesome family commitments.

To be fully creative in Christian terms, such a development must involve explicit occasions and experiences of worship and celebration, shared moments of meaning in which "the Beyond in our midst" is acknowledged, a "practicing of the presence" in both inter-human and transcendental dimensions, provision for "the great conversation" about life's fundamental issues in the light of Christian revelation, opportunities for group meditation and prayer, sharing and bible study, and a wrestling with the meaning of Christian love and discipleship for the fateful social issues of our time. In the congregation I know best a tradition of family camping, in a mode that provides for serious encounter and that encompasses large numbers of the congregation, has furthered and undergirded over the past twenty years a network of family relationships in terms as those I have just described.

One of the life-transforming meanings of the Christian faith is that we may participate now in a quality of life that is eternal; the love which was given definitive expression in Jesus Christ and which is "of God" is known at a depth of our experience. At the same time, pervasive moral ambiguity continues to characterize our existence and our life together as Christians. The enlivening new state of being we experience is still but a foretaste, an earnest, of "the powers of the age to come."

It is partly because our lives remain contingent and incomplete that the Christian revelation is such extraordinary "good news"! Jesus Christ emboldens us to affirm that the power upon which all human beings are dependent for the ultimate completion of their lives is holy love! Speaking of the human pilgrimage, the Book of Hebrews declares, "Here we find no continuing city" — no abiding home! The very fact that we undertake efforts that will not be completed in history and yet that we live as though the frame of life's meaning is wider than nature and time, points to the faith, hope and love which inspire our striving!

Gilbert Chesterton expressed memorably the paradox of faith in a Reality that is present as well as future, transformingly experienced now but not bound indissolubly to any achieved good. In his poem, "The House of Christmas," Chesterton wrote:

"For men are homesick in their homes,
   And strangers under the sun,
And they lay their heads in a foreign land
   Whenever the day is done . . .
To an open house in the evening
   Home shall men come,
To an older place than Eden
   And a taller town than Rome.
To the end of the way of the
   wandering star,
To the things that cannot be
   and that are,
To the place where He was homeless
   And all men are at home!"

I Am A Surgeon

By MARK SNYDER, M.D.
YAKIMA, WASHINGTON

I am a Surgeon — A surgeon who works on the central core of the human organism, the heart, the lungs, and the blood vessels. One does not become a surgeon unless he wants to very badly. My talents may or may not be greater than anybody else's, but it is clear that I wanted to do this thing more than anything else. I state matter of factly that I have worked harder at my profession than you have at yours. A colleague of mine expressed the expenditures of his energies when he said, "It possessed me so much I traded it for my youth". In many ways it has been the joining of a priesthood, a young priesthood, for significant surgical treatment has come to human civilization only in the last one hundred years. Surgery has been among the most demanding in licensure and tightly controlled of the disciplines that man undertakes. Indeed, with an uninterrputed continuance of training, I, myself, had spent the midpoint of my life before I became an independent operator. The cornerstones of my profession have, first of all, been the determination — the commitment. A realization and dedication to excellence. The maintenance and application of expertness.

Like most of you, I also am a seminarian. I am closely involved with the actuality of life. I differ in that I am a physical seminarian, a human mechanic. I am occupied at the crisis points of the human phenomena of life. I am concerned with existence.

Living matter is an internal organization of sustaining energy. Man is a summation, an evolutionary pyramidization, of primative unicellular energy. The gradual diversification into complex systems of organ function lead finally to the composite identity of man. His intricate organization has had all the pragmatic deliberation of time; there has been little recognizable model change in the last 25,000 years. The human body, microscopically, is a system mass of operative living cellular units. These cellular units are the only component blessed with life. They perform in a precoded, predictable, integrated fashion. There are an infinite number of variations in human injury and bodily malfunction which, nonetheless, tend to be comprehendable in orderly patterns. To prick a single cell amoeba is to observe a protoplasmic coagulum in withdrawal. To enter the human organism with a scalpel is to intitiate the star spangled explosion of action, reaction and interaction. The momentum of the effect becomes undeniable. Each individual cell, as a unit and as a composite member, sends forth its own raindrop into a cascade of bodily response. The internal energy system process can be momentarily tempered, swerved, and supported; it cannot be created.

The essence of the surgical occupation, then, is an endeavor within the realities of physical laws and human process. The surgeon's job is to comprehend, in its myriad of detail, the human life process, and to perceive in specific situations how this is being interrupted, with hope to reconstitute a favorable environment for continuance. One's only choice, the only reality, is in the process of rapprochement.

Within man's physical workings there coexists unparalleled harmony and synchrony in tenuous chemical and anatomical proximity to disaster. An example might well be the 2 mm. thickness of the wall of the large bowel. This composite, membranous band separates the delicate, sterile, internal milieu of the body from the life-threatening bacteria and toxins swarming within the bowel lumen. Thus, human physcial existence is a myriad of interfaces between comparative and conflicting environments. The anatomic and molecular building blocks of these environments and their laws of chemical and physical reaction are on both sides of the interface, identical. Life depends on this integrated series of delicate packages, separated yet contained within the structure and function of crucial membranes. It is into this great proximity of integrity of structure and function versus impending degradation and demise that the transient quality of health is defined. It is here that the surgeon lives. It is at this anatomic interface and this moment of time that the surgeon exists. He lives at the point of confrontation.

Let us consider the patient Sam Jones. Mr. Jones has never seen the essence of his surgeon. He has not come to me necessarily because I am a good person; nonetheless, we have made a mutual statement about his priorities. I have given Mr. Jones a commitment. All attention is now undivided. Sam Jones is at moment. My personal and collective unity are now at moment. My singular existence, my phenomena, will remain in the workshop while its produce will become known. Mr. Jones is at risk and is to become a future, an outcome. As the orchestration is begun, the identity of Mr. Jones is diffused. His person submerges into that of a teeming life system, a representative of the species, an internal, living, pulsating life system which will be opened and placed in a state of urgency. An aggressive invasion has been wrought. This is not a willy-nilly affair. Fine lines between harmony and disaster are to be caressed. What a great disappointment if only the surgeon's brow is moist, if only surgeon's pulse is elevated. Should there not be some physical gesture of acknowledgement — some snowflake somewhere — to give this moment its due? At this table now is the excitement and imperativeness of man's human experience. This human physical system has a very rapid feedback process. It is uniquely satisfying, comforting, terrorizing, that when the aggression has begun, this same system will get better or worse in a very short interval of time.

The surgeon's toil becomes the confrontation of man's existence. It is a very personal, yet collective urgency. To the surgeon, however, the experience remains intensely singular. His judgments and responsibilities are critically personal. Alone, he is responsible to all critieria of performance. The scapel, the clamps, the sewing needles become extensions of his personal being. He is under the gun and forced to make a statement, a statement which will be tested. The outcome becomes open for judgment by all. In my mind's eye and with the sweat of my brow I see it little differently from primitive man facing a tiger with a spear in his hand.

There is a great security and profoundness in being held accountable — the human spirit craves it. Certainly one of life's great necessities is to be held accountable.

Maturation brings to all the opportunity to comprehend man's individual and social behaviour — his humanness. The surgical perspective adds three further dimensions:

First is the revelation and insight of sincerity and oneness which reflects in man's actions and visage at points of crises. There emerges a picture of basic man — of man threatened with existence. It is a moment of modulation when all the static is discarded — the apparel is shed and basic decisions and choices are capable of being made. The tea is gone and there remains the realities of the leaves. A crisis to a surgeon is a studied and practiced discipline which is intended to have an outcome — an effect. By the uniqueness of his stance and the challenging turmoil of his environment I would surmise that a surgeon should have a pretty good start at being a basic man — that is if he is not shackled by his own authority.

Second is the surgical overview on process. As a surgeon I have come to know death. I have watched the inalienable chemical and physical process within a living organism quiver when it can no longer find its equilibrium. I have watched the unitizing, formulative force, representative of the species and the uniqueness of the individual, be dissipated. I have seen the positive charge, the spark, the energizing organization escape. I have held the human heart in my hands as it has grown still. I have felt a myriad of tender individual environment cease. I have watched the privilege of the moment to be lost. I have seen an operative plan fail, an idea drown in its adversity to the realities of physical process, a technical maneuver bleed to disaster. Nonetheless, through all of this, the meaning, the spirit of life is intensified.

I have also known birth. I have felt the re-equilibration of protoplasmic activity dawn on a human face. I have seen birth as a moment of insight, a realization which allows change in performance. I know it as a person freed of a physical impairment. I know birth as an idea, an innovation, a solution to a difficult problem which has real outcome and existence.

Thirdly, through the elemental care of people of all ages, has come the awareness of man in all of his seasons. The ability to look at a person and picture him as a member of the family of man; in his childhood, in middle age, and in the elder years. To gaze at a boy's mannerism and extrapolate this into its visage at maturity. To see and understand the pristine beauty of youthful structure and function as developmental to the adapted, responded and scarred structure of the adult. To look at an elderly grin and see it in its infancy. To look at a person and deja vu his existence is a beautiful baseline for understanding. To obtain the overview of the human experience in all of its decades and as a completed unit. To conceptualize the totality of man's experience in life.

The total phenomena of surgery has traditionally been an expression of the Christian ethic. It has been a working model of the philosophy of the rights of the individual to personal choice, to individual existence — come what may. But what of the worldwide species overview of man in 1977 relative to the surgical endeavor? The application of surgery to human disease has developed to the point where it is now pressing the available limits of economic energy. I have expended years of training and effort to be able to insert an artificial heart valve into middle aged and elderly patients. The hospital charges for this single event are astronomical. Life is extended and some degree of augmentation of function is obtained. There are a moderate number of people whose productivity is augmented. With the social energy resource environment of World 1977 this has to be examined. This has to be contrasted to the large number of humans who need basic nutritional support and a primary immunizations for preventable disease. All of this latter at a fraction of the cost relegated to ultrasophisticated surgical endeavors such as kidney transplantation, facial cosmesis, and some forms of cardiac surgery.

In my little baliwick, I continue to be primarily concerned with what to do and how to do it. The real pressing daily issue coming to hand is: What is basic human existence? What is ordinary versus extraordinary in human life? We are being forced to consider the quality and longevity of restored lifespan in the decision making process. As the truth of economic feasibility, or energy expenditure, collide with a rapidly escalating population base, the realities of a new functional ethic are arising. The singular concept of existence is under pressure for modification. On a one-on-one practical, everyday basis, this is a conundrum. This ethic must be concerned with individual obligation rather than with individual right.

I would prophesy the development of indices of community or human productivity. These indices will be used as modifying factors when one comes to formulate the treatment regimen. A specific medical situation will call for widely different treatment plans based on social criteria. In effect, all individuals will not have equal access to life support and technological facility. The realities of energy expenditure are now at hand and they will challenge the traditional American luxury of individual rights and personal liberty. Surgery, then, particularly at this moment, is a very exciting field. Its technical applications and human salvage are burgeoning. It is currently at the forefront of synthesis and expression of new dilemmas in human and moral ethical obligation. It is a unique window into mankind.

In summary, let us re-examine the core statement of a core surgeon:

> MY PRIMAL WARMTH IS IN MY ALIGNMENT WITH THE LIFE PROCESS AND THE INGREDIENTS OF THE UNIVERSE.
>
> THE PRIVILEGE OF BEING FUNCTIONALLY ALIVE AMONG OTHER RESPONSIBLE PEOPLE IN THE WORLD WHO ARE MAKING HUMANITY RUN.
>
> THE PARTICIPATION IN A HUMAN ENDEAVOR OF GREAT MAGNITUDE WHICH HAS BEEN FOUGHT BY EVERY GENERATION AND WHICH REFLECTS THE ON-GOINGNESS OF OUR HUMAN SOCIETY.
>
> THE ORCHESTRATION OF A REMEDY AND THE GIVING OF COMFORT.
>
> MY TITILLATION HAS BEEN TO BE ABLE TO ENTER, HARMONIZE, RESTRUCTURE, PALLIATE WITHIN MANKIND'S LIFE SYSTEM — MY HUMANNESS IS TO HAVE BEEN TICKLED PINK AT GETTING AWAY WITH IT!

**Images
Containing
Futures**

CONCEPTUALIZED PRIMORDIALS

People do not need to know everything.
They do need to experience a few things they can depend upon . . . an Inner-Personal Region. some bit of earth that can be transformed into meaningful world. A Thou and an I.
A religious style of life concentrates on a few primordials.
Not upon a scatter of bits of good advice . . . or an overload of information that comes and goes, drugging our minds each hour on the hour . . . or upon "busywork"
"Somehow I have a sense that there is something basic about myself that I'm not really dealing with"

1.

A **primordial** is a "Beginning of beginnings". A primordial keeps on turning out beginnings. (It is not just something that **first** happened)
  Primeval ooze is a primordial. *As you look at a marsh in the spring. fermenting with the suns help. do not hold it in disdain. For out of the marshes of the good earth, some beginnings of you and I crawled out millenia ago. And who knows what is going on there now?*
  Ecology of Spirit *is another primordial. For it is out of such ecology that human spirit takes form. And becomes forever "Exuberance rushing into Significant Form"*
  Spirit *is a primordial. The beginning of every new social movement is a surging ocean of spirit . . . within people.*
  Primordials of individual human existence are such goings on as I-Thou. generativity, the Inner-Personal, symbolizing, interiorizing other persons, congregation, home place, the mating of future-past-present whose offspring is new futures, death, birth.
  Primordials are Forming Forms . . . Forms of great potential needing only awakening, nurturing, and an identity to keep them connected together as an organism and heading in some direction.
  A primordial is a developmental power . . . that is a gift from the emergent evolution of the species. Capable of making the individual a member of the species.
  However a primordial is not just something that happened first archeologically. It is fundament, seed, roots, tree now.

2.

And what is conceptualizing?

Conceptualizing is seeing beneath the visual surface which one can stroke . . . into the organizing pattern of "elephant." And then painting in our consciousness a picture of elephant such as a Van Gogh would . . . of the **system of energies** *which are making elephant.*

Every concept is a **system** *of ideas, not just one idea. A family of ideas that speed each other up to the speed of light. A concept is a somewhat well-rounded understanding of the working thrust, design, and possibility of "the marsh" we are participating in. Marsh, not as a conglomerate of this and that, but as a field of creation and emergence.*

Further, in conceptualizing, we go for the DNA and a synopsis of the script of development meaningful.

Every "grand" concept" is a vortex . . . swirling up residues of the past, sucking in immediacies of the present, roaring toward New Time and a world it makes.

Therefore, to conceptualize something human, we must bring together the intellectual, the artistic, the religious ways of knowing. Conceptualizing is an act of the full orb of consciousness.

But a concept does emphasize intellectual symbolizing. We are not primarily possessed by "I feel" "I hunger" "I didn't care" "I remember".

3.

Conceptualized primordials are prime agents of the emergence of humankind. And of human culture.

Treasure the existence of conceptualized primordials in your mind and in the mind of your congregation.

Why fool around with symptoms and trifles when you can be dealing with the Beginning of beginnings?

**Images
Containing Futures**

III
Celebrative Education
FORMING FORM

1.

Form is not a mold for jello . . . a structure into which we relax.

Form is something that intends something
   Emerging, driving forward
      Mobilizing itself as it goes along

Form is not a finished structure, but a powerfully coded pattern of energy.

Form is what a seed is. What coded DNA is.

Sperm and egg do not contain a miniature human body, but coding energies.

2.

Form is always FORMING FORM. Exuberance on its way to Significant Form. All the systems are set to go.

   A live body is form
      A cadaver is not
   A cadaver is disintegrating structure.

Form is the disciplined alert football player who instantaneously combines his body and the opposing team into an opening thru which he goes. Meeting stonewall straight ahead, he twists to the left where he feels the soft spot, and gains three more yards.

"Conditioned to do just one thing" is not form.

Form "completes the good curve" in novel situations. Calls up next possibilities. Selects which one is completion.

And the meaning burgeons.

Form is Frank Lloyd Wright's mind inventing buildings fit for American traditions. But if he had never built a building, his mind would not have been a form, but a dream that flees with predawn's arrival.

Form is a Beethoven piano concerto. Plus its re-creating Forming Form in our consciousness each time it is played.

Form is a Pentecost congregation caught up in intense revelation . . . until together they speak a language which humankind everywhere can understand.

3.

Form . . .
A field of tensions bound together by a common destiny.
An integrity that has "put it all together"
    doing something directly and well
        the inevitable right cadence, right word flows and much more will unexpectedly happen
Whatever is done, is done . . .
    without crippling reservations, doublemindedness, half-heartedness.
Form is not a menagerie . . .
    but a loving coherence
        a creative fidelity to the growth of the **whole.**
Form is music, not a single note by itself.
A laissez-faire church is not a FORM. A merely pluralistic country is not a form.
In a way, Forming Form is everything! Without it we are a nothing . . . or soon will be.

4.

Form can renew itself. Come up with a freshness. Change tactics within a strategy.

A developmental saga.
    "More truth and light is yet to break forth" from the Beginning of beginnings.
    Hunger for pragnanz eliminates the clutter
    The impacts of new history bring out still partially-hidden powers.
    "That which does not kill me, strengthens me."

Transcendence
    The pupa, long-developing, becomes the monarch butterfly which will make the long, long journey. With a new name and identity.

5.

"I praise aloud the thought well-thought, the deed well-done" the person who is a strong statement of their truth. For all these have such greater power to fascinate . . . and to shape further thoughts/worlds . . ". than can the feebly middling.

Education is concerned with Forming Form. Not with handing around cadavers . . . or feeling generally wistful. Developmental and history-making education has little place for energies that remain ghosts and angels . . . and never become bodied, substantiated, **forming** forms.

In particular, religious education and the church are concerned not with just any idea, but with meanings, vision, ideas, a mode of consciousness . . . that are **generative of many ideas and enterprises.** Generative of the Species Humankind.

    We would teach the living tree, not a pile of sawdust.
Spirit is pro-creative.

The Intentional Sapling

By RICHARD FISHER
C.T.S.

A few weeks ago, on a bright Sunday morning, I met a 200 year old American lion in our 4th and 5th grade Sunday School class. He told us of witnessing the Revolutionary War of 1776, the American Civil War, Viet Nam and as if this wasn't enough mayhem, he told us of the murders and executing of Garry Gilmore. While he spoke a young fiddler sat on the branch of a tree playing his viola, interpreting the words and feelings to our astonished and frightened group.

If you'd been there observing, you'd probably just have seen a typical group of wide-eyed children watching and listening to two of their own species play-acting. But if that is all you saw and heard, it is because you had forgotten to don your hat of imagination. You didn't see that we were really sitting in a dense forest, around an old stump of a tree sharing and trying to make sense of some bleak turbulent experiences — some Dark Moments — of an old lion and a fiddler in a tree. This group was about something significant: Understanding and reconciling the reality of suffering, injustice and death with the reality of our peaceful forest home, our forest of many trees and the gurgling never-ending brook.

For the past year I have been working on an image-model of Christian Education. As the Director of Christian Education in a suburban Episcopal Church, I soon concluded that any meaningful vision would have to come from the actual lives of the children attending the Church School, as these childrens' lives encountered the Church. So I climbed down out of my office and books and joined my wife in leading a 4th and 5th grade class. We began with some hunches gleaned from our theological, psychological, educational phenomenological mentors. These hunches dwelled within the fertile inheritance of our faith/tradition mixing with the ever new ground of our own lived-experience (individual and communal). They seem to me to be the DNA of the learning process, especially as it is focused on Christian Education. They describe three mountains which rise from an ancient valley of Spirit: BEING-in relationship, or the existential, ethical relationship of God to person, person to God and person to person; the COGNITIVE dimensions of our full Judeo-Christian faith/tradition; and the ARTING mode of incarnating. Into this horizon we walked in the early morning light like young shepherds with a flock, constantly asking, "What did we see? What did it mean?" The answers we hoped gave us the Life-World of the children, which in turn told us more about those we were 'being' with.

The Life-World model for understanding a child (person) has been systematically developed and taught by Ross and Martha Snyder at Chicago Theological Seminary. We use it as the existential basis for teaching; as a key in living out "The Second Great Commandment", as the human relational context for the "First".

I want to share with you now our experience of Life-Worlds encountering the structures of our faith/tradition in an arting process. I want to come back to that 200 year old American lion and the possibilities of that forest and the gurgling stream. My tactic will be to bring you through the creating of this enterprise as if you were there-present.

We have been in the classroom together now 15 minutes. You are my team-teaching partner. We have been setting up paint jars and paper a-plenty. We've already discussed the nuts and bolts of our class intention. We want to begin a long term project that can give the children the experience of affirmation in the context of the caring group. We want them to experience love and empowering concern under the conditions of an imperfect human existence, yet a truly HUMAN EXISTENCE fired by Emmanuel (God is with us); and hence, a human existence that lives in awe, wonder, mystery and hope. Theologically, we think we are attempting to point to, to recognize and to participate in the Kingdom of God. Our specific theme, or tradition-bearing-concept, is taken from the Biblical reading of the week according to the Episcopal Church Propers. It is "The Blessed of the Lord." It comes from the 1st Psalm, our text; its second stanza is our focus: "A tree planted by streams of water bringing forth fruit in its season." As we worked with the Propers this week we kept in mind the developmental limits and abilities of the persons we teach. These resources helped us build a strategy for communicating the cognitive dimension of our task. We knew of these childrens' need for concrete images, their limited ability at space/time conceptualization (or abstraction), their intense power of imagination and their movement into more reciprocal peer relationships. The tree-image of the 1st Psalm was a fortuitous presence for helping our 10 to 12 year olds understand what, who and how is "The Blessed of the Lord.": "A tree-planted by waters, bringing forth fruit, its branches ever leafy." And by coincidence, we had a deep psychic symbol that could tell us a lot about the inner Life-Worlds of the children, From whatever happened today in class, we could structure new classes to enable the children become full-functioning centers of freedom and love: i.e. Children of God.

But this is all background, memories of what we have already done and thought together, and the room is now filling with 7 children who want our presence present. So we shift our concentration and begin.

We share hellos and a brief round of the past week's highlights (possible Lived-Moments?). Then I ask the kids to "Draw yourself as a tree. What kind of a tree would you look like if you were a tree right now, this very moment. Hurry! Draw yourself as a tree!"

As trees take shape on the papers, you take up the Bible and read the first Psalm. When the trees are pretty much completed, you read back over the second verse:

> He is like a tree that is planted
> by water streams,
> yielding its fruit in season,
> its leaves never fading;
> success attends all he does.

I say, "Now if you were a new tree, a tree planted by such streams of living water; if you were such a tree bursting forth fruit and ever leafy, what would you look like? Draw yourself now as such a new tree."

So, the children begin drawing themselves as a new tree. There are the inevitable hassels to keep us jumping. Paint brushes being swiped and fought over, declarations to never stand next to a girl again, shouting matches between two needy contestants . . . in other words, a lot of UNDERSTANDING to help with . . . in other words, a lot of GROWING being worked on.

In these pictures we can see some subtle transformations, some difference in the two sets of trees; there are clues everywhere, in the lean of the trunks, the thrust of the bushy tops, the thickness or thinness of the brush strokes: They are all potential clues to the Life-World of the child and indications of growings that are not even in the bud stage yet. But we see their possibility there and we burn with excitement. And due to the wholistic nature of arting, we can trust that the transformations on paper point to the experience within the person/artist.

With the second set of trees completed, we have everyone, including ourselves, for we too painted, bring the pictures together. We create a forest, a community. And we listen as each tree shares some words about its life if it wants to. We talk about what it is like to be such and such a tree, and what it is like to be a forest. We talk about things to do in the forest, about travels we could take, things we could do to care for it or how we might destroy it with a careless unintentional match.

We then put our trees up on a wall of our room. We paint a river running through it, each child taking a section of the river to add. Then we adjourn, telling them that next Sunday we will take a trip through our forest together, an imaginative journey we will embellish with mime-drama.

In a few minutes we meet again in the church sanctuary. But now we are all part of the larger community. They meet me in a new role, as an important leader, dressed in our tradition's vestment, administering the cup at communion. They probably kneel next to you at the rail.

After the service, you and I join the other teachers in my office for a Reflection Group. We focus our attention upon the Life-World of the children in our respective classes. In our turn, we share some insights we've picked up from this sequence of pictures which they have made today.

A week passes; we have pooled and questioned our observations and we design a new class; Lent is now the church season and the dark week is drawing near. Our idea is to lead them on a scary trip into the forest; and at the reflection group we tell the other teachers, and clarify ourselves, what happened, of how we met a 200 year old lion and a fiddler.

A couple of teachers say it is amazing that this class of previously unruly and difficult kids are having this kind of cooperative experience together. One teacher, a close friend of the fiddler, frankly states: "That child has been a real terror in that family; hard to control, disruptive, probably hyperactive and just basically impossible to deal with unless you bear down hard which they, and most everyone else, does."

Well, we say, he decided to bring his viola in last week. He said nothing to the whole class after we invited him to play. He spoke no word, yet WORD came through his music. He sat on a branch of a tree and as the rest of us acted out our trip into the forest, he became the interpreter. When we met the lion he fiddled sounds while the lion spoke, sounds that echoed and amplified the tales of horror the old American lion told. When we finally left the forest and returned to our classroom, we knew that we'd met a very ancient lion and a very new song.

The project we began continues. Each week we take new trips fueled by imagination and guided by the texts and meanings of our faith/tradition. After the journeys, we continue to art the significant moments of these experiences and add them to our forest wall. These images, now moving toward symbol, will eventually be planted by us on a large banner. The banner will then hang on a prominent wall of our church building. It is a contribution of the saplings to the forest.

The slides (the children's pictures of themselves as trees in the first exercise have now been photographed and mounted as color slides), I think, offer us a paradigmatic image of the redemptive power/presence of God in our midst, working in our own rather seemingly mundane existence. The task of interpreting them as such is a process of contemporary theologizing. From the point of view of both the children initially creating and then the teachers/adults appreciatively encountering the paintings and banner and working to make meaning of them (theologizing) is a clear image of what Christian Education can be.

Secondly, the power of art to collaborate with the essential learning process, of combining concept with incarnate truth, is demonstrated.

Thirdly, we have a good example of one way of how "the Bible speaks" to people. The power of biblical images to affect a graceful transformation, in a brief time, given the right circumstances, is also demonstrated.

Fourthly, the process by which a person learns significant "content", the great demand of our "curricularists", is exemplified. It is content personally appropriated by both the individual and the group. With these kinds of learnings, I feel that the process gives us all a significant opening into ministry.

For The Religious Hunger of Inner City Children

By DAVID B. HENRY
4th Congregational, Chicago

Until just a few years ago, the Church School at Fourth Church got along reasonably well, conducting itself as it had for perhaps the last thirty or forty years. It was structured very much like the great "Sunday Schools" of the past, with its own independent treasury and mission fund and governing board. Its membership had been composed primarily of the children of members and friends of the church, who began their church involvement there, and grew up knowing the customs and practices of the Church School. They learned early on that worship is a time for quiet, and class sessions are a time to listen, whether or not the material at hand is of interest.

Lately, however, this situation has changed. The Church School has seen an increase in the number of children whose parents have no formal relationship, and little or no actual relationship to the church. Due to the existence of a community youth program conducted by the church, and to other factors such as the rapid transition the community is in, children were beginning to enter the system at any age, from Primary to Senior High, to be more and more unfamiliar with the "unwritten rules" of the Church School, and to feel very free to act out their interest or disinterest in the material accordingly. Equally, they brought with them many of the special needs and problems of children in their community, those associated with poverty and actually or functionally absent parents.

With the influx of these children over a period of time, the teachers found themselves facing more and more difficulties in even maintaining the order they had been accustomed to. Variety in the class sessions was sacrificed in the interest of "getting through" the lesson for the day. The material they had been using relied heavily on the student's ability to read, and, with reading levels well below those normally associated with grade-school children, the students often struggled through the written material, word by word, oblivious to the meaning of that being read. Inattentiveness was the rule, and verbal battles and even outright fistfights between the children were becoming more and more common.

Several cosmetic changes in the sessions were tried, but they failed to rectify the difficulties. Finally, it became clear to the teachers and to me, that some other, long-range kinds of attention were needed.

This "attention" concentrated itself in two areas, one being the development of different curriculum material, more suited to the needs of the children in the area, and the other being several teacher workshops to explore the needs of the children, the functioning of the Church School and the nature of Christian Education.

It became clear to us from the outset that the operation of the Church School could not depend of the children's pre-conceived notions about, or respect for the church itself or the Church School. That is to say that our legitimacy, as far as the children were concerned, would depend on the extent to which we fulfilled their need and longings.

It was with this realization that Ross Snyder's concept of Religious Hunger became important. In the past, the first question addressed by the teacher in planning was, "What must I teach this quarter?" Beginning with the notion of religious hunger, however, our starting point became, "What would be Good News to the children?" The development of curriculum and dialogue with the teachers began to center around the search for the entity in their environment to which their deepest needs for meaning were directed.

Briefly stated, the "questions" which Ross Snyder associates with Religious Hunger are as follows:
1. Is it possible to put together a world which I can Live?
2. Is there a power that can overcome and transform the destruction that keeps coming at me?
3. Will I ever realize myself?
4. Is there a warm body of people who believe in each other and in something together — in which I could be a first-class citizen?

We found that the street culture, and the street gang in particular was a source of meaning for these children. Although few children of the age that were involved in the Church School were actually involved in the organized gangs of the area, their language and actions reflected the importance of the image of the gang to them. (I remember refereeing a battle between two six-year-olds who threatened to get their "gangs" after each other. Neither knew what they were fighting about, or had any real interest in fighting. Both, however, felt very good about having a "gang" to call upon.) The image of the gang provided, for these children, a world to live . . . a nomos with its own values, secret signs and rituals and mysteries. For the children in our neighborhood, the gang provides a sense of power for the powerless, protection and safety amid the dangers of their world. It provides a group of people who believe in each other, and an opportunity to say, "I am somebody".

In light of this, our Church School took "The Jesus Gang" as its theme. The curriculum material I had been designing was reworked to tell the story of Jesus and His disciples in terms that would be understandable to the children's orientation to the gang culture. The vision of the Church School as a "congregation" or a "band of persons" was emphasized over its aspects as a "school". The sharing of lived moments, between students and teachers became a central aspect. Sessions began with the sharing of experiences related to the story for the day (e.g., "rejection" in relation to the story of Jesus at Nazareth in Luke), moved to a telling of the story and then to the birthing of meanings from the shared experiences and the story. Sessions culminated with an activity open-ended enough that meanings discovered in the sessions could be incorporated, and worship.

Worship became the responsibility of the classes in turns, not a single leader, and the classes were encouraged to share the meanings they had discovered through various media.

This is still an experiment in-process, and it is impossible as yet to make any final judgement on its value for the Church School. However, it has gone well. Many of the behaviour problems which first prompted attention to the Church School have subsided, others have not. At the last teachers' meeting, the request was made that the material be continued beyond the original date for the termination of the experiment. There is a growing feeling of community in the Church School, and greater interest on the parts of the students in its life.

Building a Congregation Through Intergenerational Celebration

TOM CHULAK, C.T.S.

Within our society and its institutions, a gap has developed between the young children, young adults, adults and elderly. The extended family and intergenerational neighborhoods of the past are no longer an actuality within most communities. Mobility has helped to split the ages.

This segregation based on age is disastrous for our culture. It denies our children the wisdom of the elderly; it denies the elderly the bright eyes and inquisitiveness of the child, and it cuts adults off from youth and youth off from adults.

It is the premise of this paper that one of the best institutions to address age segregation is the church. The church is one of the few communities that has within it persons of all ages who come together regularly in hopes of building a congregation. A place where persons of all ages interact with one another in their quest for meaning.

As a result of my concern with this problem, I began to explore significant ways in which this segregation could be broken within the church community. This exploration developed into a model of intergenerational celebration that opens up the possibility for increased interaction between the ages.

THE ORIGINATING EXPERIENCE

In late October, 1976, a group of 5 children ranging from ages 6-18, two adults and I met to plan a Christmas celebration focusing on the meaning of Christmas. The participants were asked to take one experience that had been meaningful to them in Christmases of the past. Those who were old enough to put their experiences into writing did so. The younger children verbally expressed their experiences and I wrote them down. One little girl of six said, "to me the reading of **Twas the Night Before Christmas** is the most important." A boy of eight said, "a trip to my grandma's in Iowa was the best Christmas I every had, my uncle and I played together much of the time." Another boy talked of a watch he had received as a present and one of the adults described how it felt to be part of the family reunion just after he and his brother had returned from the Viet Nam war.

These experiences were a starting point for exploring their meaning in greater depth. After searching for the significance of each experience expressed we then grouped those experiences that were similar enough to be looked at together. The grouped experiences were then named, thereby symbolizing these experiences through a word or two. The named experiences were then integrated with appropriate traditions of Christmas. The final step was to put the intergenerational celebration into significant form. This final form included the lived experiences, narrative, story, poetry, and tradition.

This celebration had come out of the hearts of people of all ages. This intergenerational celebration didn't just plug children and adults into an order of service but was truly an expression of those who participated. It was an expression emerging from the congregation and not just one person. It had depth and breadth and was presented on the first Sunday of December, 1976.

Following the service a woman came up to me and stated "you have expressed what I have felt inside for a long time," another said "for years we have tried to include our children in our worship but this for me was the first time it has succeeded." Other comments made me belive that there was power in this model.

THE EMERGING THEORY

With this background of an actual experience, let us explore the theory and concepts behind this model. Underlying this model is the conviction that Religious Institutions should be concerned with building a congregation, and that intergenerational celebration can be an aid in that process.

Using Richard Niebur, Ross Snyder and Martin Buber as sources I would define a congregation in the following way. It is a group of people who voluntarily gather together for the purpose of increasing among themselves the love of God and of fellow human beings; they believe in each other and in something together; they stand in living mutual relationship to a single living center and stand in relationship to one another; and they are in search of a home.

At the heart of love, belief, relationship, home, and therefore at the heart of a congregation is the need for a process of communication which allows for meaningful interaction between members of the congregation. Communication necessitates a symbolic system of meaning through which persons can be understood one by another and thereby create mutuality. Therefore if one is attempting to build a congregation then a system of common symbols and meanings must be developed.

If you will agree that communication, significant symbol, and their corresponding meanings are essential to building a congregation, then the method or process by which the symbols take on meaning within the congregation becomes crucial.

This is the point at which the theory of intergenerational celebration becomes important, for it is through celebration that significant symbol can emerge within a congregation. Celebration, as used here, is referring to the process whereby:

1) An experience or lived moment is described (e.g. the 8 experiences of Christmas).
2) These moments of experience are then transformed and intensified into meaning and symbol (e.g. in the Christmas celebration the process of exploring the experiences and naming them).
3) The experiences are then related to the tradition.
4) The experiences in conjunction with the tradition are put into significant form which is then communicated to the congregation (e.g. the use of multi-dimensional communication forms).
5) The communication of the symbol and its meaning is embodied by the people thereby creating inter-subjectivity. This implies the celebration occurs only when the communication of the symbol has been embodied (e.g. the woman's comment after the service).

Celebration within the congregational setting is therefore concerned with intensifying, transforming and creating symbols that vibrate with significance for the people.

Celebration, used in a general context, can happen in any situation in which two or more people gather. However, for the purposes of the model of intergenerational celebration is it necessary to narrow this concept of celebration to those situations which are created and performed by persons of varying age levels and communicated to persons of different age levels. Rather than a one person celebration, this style is created corporately by different aged people.

OPENINGS INTO THE CONGREGATION

The power of intergenerational celebration lies in the fact that: 1) The celebration has emerged out of a cross section of age groups within the congregation. This allows for significant intergenerational communication. 2) The celebration is communicated in such a way that the total congregation participates, thereby giving the children, youth, and adults both young and old a significant common experience. 3) This approach combines the process of education through phenomenology with our worship of the community. In other words what emerges out of the educational process is used as the basis for celebration. 4) Through the exploring of the relationship between experiences and the tradition the opportunity has been opened for all age groups to theologize, and 5) From this process significant symbol is lifted up for the congregation to embody.

It must be made clear that one need not start with general experience as was done in the Christmas celebration. One could just as easily create an intergenerational celebration based on the life of a significant person, an event experienced by the whole congregation, or an event in history or tradition.

This model also need not be restricted to a church but could be used in any intergenerational situation. It was also not meant as a model that could be used each Sunday in a church, but as one that could happen 3 or 4 times a year.

Celebration is spirited powerful energies being released within a congregation whose hope is the creation of symbols and meanings that become a habitat for the people of the congregation. These symbols become a part of the home in which people dwell. All of us in our struggle to be human are hungry for meaningful expressions that lead to a life that is trustworthy.

THE MEMORABLE IMAGE

Imagine eight people sitting before a congregation of approximately 100. Together we have spent six weeks struggling to express ourselves. I am sitting in the fourth seat from left, at my right is a girl of 6 who has bought a new pair of black shoes especially for the celebration. For the past three weeks she has been practicing reading **Twas the Night Before Christmas.** On my left is a boy of 8 who has in his hand a written testimony about his trip to his grandmother's. In the other chair on my right is the man who struggled to express what it felt like to return home from Viet Nam and be reunited with his family at Christmas time. There is the high school girl who has practiced singing "O Holy Night" a capella. There I am struggling to find the words to express how it feels to sing carols on Christmas eve with my family. Out of our struggle for meaning together we come before this congregation hoping within our hearts to be able to say what is within us. Hoping to offer new meaning to the symbol of Christmas. Before us is the congregation who don't know what we have been through together, but who will only experience the finished product. In the congregation is a woman who has come to see her son participate in the celebration and who is thankful that he has been included in the significant life of the church. Others come expecting a disoriented presentation with children having to be cued on where to stand and what to say. The eight of us are in the front of the sanctuary, and the congregation is sitting on chairs. Our hope is that together we can indwell one another, thereby lifting all of us to new life as a congregation.

Wonder As Sacrament

By PAUL WRIGHTMAN
Sacred Heart Church, Medford, Oregon

Kierkegaard says somewhere that the way in which we begin a journey pretty much sets our destination. My hunch is that if we begin with the notion of wonder we will wind up with the reality of sacrament. In broad outline, I see this process as follows:

Wonder — inescapable, irresistible, yearning-burning hidden in our depths. Drawing us out of ourselves, our shells, pulling-pushing us into our uniqueness. Sparking some to symphonies, some to children, some to words of print or paint or play, some to passing on tradition (reverently, as a handful of light). And whispering some to magnificent inconspicuousness. Through these thousand simple-complex acts flows our common human longing to reach out and touch that which we sense to be the still point of the turning story of our lives — God.

And God, out of breath, as it were, after singing the mysterious song of becoming at the center of each being, rested, exulting in the goodness of creation. Yet — dare one speak this way about the Creator of the Universe — God, too, felt a nameless yearning: not just to be the center, but to be an I for every Thou. And God reached out in longing and created what we call a sacrament, that relationship of wholeness — holiness — that occurs when Creator meets creature.

God reaches out in sacrament. People respond in wonder. People reach out in wonder. God responds in sacrament. Their meeting is what we call grace. "Except for the point, the still point, there would be no dance, and there is only the dance.¹"

When I began coordinating the religious education process at a large parish in southern Oregon, part of my job description was "sacramental preparation." In the Roman Catholic tradition, this typically means getting people ready for the reception of specific sacraments. In a broader context, however, this preparation is often the foundation of something much larger than the receiving of individual sacrament. Frequently, for better or worse, the approach and information a Catholic receives during these sessions is formative of their attitude toward religion — and life — in general.

In a very real sense, all of life is — or has the potential for becoming — a sacramental encounter between God and persons. In this context, "sacramental preparation" would apply to Jews and Protestants as well as Catholics. In fact — as will become apparent from my indebtedness to Abraham Joshua Heschel and Martin Buber — the Jewish tradition is uniquely in touch with wonder as sacrament. Christians have much to learn from Jews in this crucial area of spiritual development.

Preparing for the baptism of a child is an especially significant period in the life of many parents. It is one of those prime transition times of life, when adults seem more open to growth and change. It is surprising how many nominal Christians reapproach the church at the advent of a child. Obviously they are searching for something. The question I kept asking myself as a religious educator was "What do I really want to share with these people?"

Do I want to convey to them a rigid and thoroughly defined theology, or do I want to encourage them to explore their own experience and to trust that this exploration will lead them to a deeper relationship with God? Given the fact that I am committed to experience and exploration, what could be an effective way of stimulating this search in others?

In attempting to speak to this challenge, I soon came to realize that the beginning point of our exploration had to be a common, shared experience, something basic to the human condition. When I reflected on my own life experience, I discovered that a sense of wonder and mystery was fundamental.

Each of us has had the experience of being caught up in speechless admiration at the boldness of a sunset, the star-filled sky on a moonless night in the mountains, or the gentle beauty of a single flower. All of us have felt the lure of discovery, the fireworks display of insight and intuition, the yearning for something "beyond" during events of deep sorrow.

These diverse experiences share a common root in wonder, which Abraham Joshua Heschel equates with "radical amazement,[2]" Martin Buber with "abiding astonishment[3];" in other words, amazement and astonishment which originate at the very roots of our being persons. Heschel goes on to say that wonder is "the result of what man does with his higher incomprehension[4]," and ask the revealing question: "Does not mystery reign within reasoning, within perception, within explanation[5]?"

Wonder as a stance toward life enables us to see and to trust the Mystery at the root of being. It is that attitude of childlike amazement and humility which Jesus requires of his followers: "I assure you that whoever does not accept the reign of God like a little child shall not take part in it." (Mark 10:15, NAB)

Wonder is that rebirth of spirit which Jesus says is necessary for salvation:

> "I solemnly assure you,
> no one can see the reign of God
> unless he is begotten from above."
> (John 3:3, NAB)

Wonder is the realization of one's insufficiency that lies at the heart of one of the beatitudes: "How blest are those who know their need of God; the kingdom of Heaven is theirs." (Matthew 5:3, NEB)

It is characteristic of wonder that while it is perhaps the most profound of attitudes, it is also the most universal. Heschel describes this paradoxical aspect of wonder by observing that

> Radical amazement has a wider scope than any other act of man. While any act of perception or cognition has as its object a selected segment of reality, radical amazement refers to all of reality; not only to what we see, but also to the very act of seeing as well as to our own selves, to the selves that see and are amazed at their ability to see.[6]

Wonder is unique in that, unlike some of the other necessities of life, which can be withheld, it is free for the asking, present everywhere, and common to everyone.

Because, as Heschel says, "Awareness of the divine begins with wonder[7]," it only follows that endeavors in religious education need to touch base with this basic root. Especially in sessions coinciding with some of life's major events and transitions, it is crucial to enable the participants to get in touch with their own sense of wonder. What follows is a rough outline of a three session series on wonder that can set the stage for further religious education programs, especially in the areas of sacraments and values.

Parents expecting or celebrating the birth of a child, for example, are already deeply involved in the wonder of new life. During the first session, I focus on encouraging the parents to affirm their own experience of wonder.

I start by having the room reflect a sense of wonder and mystery.[8] After introductions we explore the meaning of wonder. Journals are given; everyone writes their own definition; these definitions are then anonymously read to the whole group. A lively discussion usually follows, with the leader providing direction by citing common themes and drawing attention to areas which point beyond themselves and which will be brought up in following sessions.

Next a filmstrip is shown,[9] which serves to summarize the preceding discussion and also to lead into more specific questions. Following the filmstrip we break for coffee, then go into questions such as the following:

What do you remember wondering about most as a child?
What do you wonder about most now that you're an adult?
What do you wonder about most as a prospective or actual parent?

Since many parents respond to the last question with wonderings concerning the development of their child(ren) in the area of religion and values, this question helps to lay the foundation for a future exploration of the fertile relationship between wonder and ethics. We conclude the first session with a spontaneous celebration.

The first session, then, highlights wonder as an attitude with which all the participants are familiar and are, in a sense, "experts" — because all of them have experienced wonder. Building on this shared **experience**, the first session goes on to encourage the participants to **reflect** on their experience, and then to **act** on their reflections.

In the hands of a creative facilitator, it is amazing what intuitions, insights, and inter-connections can emerge after only one evening. Common responses are: "I've never felt that my own experience counted for anything before," and "Now I'm beginning to see what it means to be a theologian, in the best sense of that word." In short, people need to have the experience of realizing that **their** experience is important.

The second session focuses on some of the implications of wonder. What are some of the elements of a vital spiritual life which flow from an active sense of wonder and mystery? I ask the participants to reflect on this question, recording their thoughts in their journals. We then share insights, my task as leader being to help shape these thoughts into a meaningful pattern. What usually emerges from our discussion are the following elements, but not necessarily in the same order. This particular pattern is one which I have found helpful.

1. Mystery and wonder lead to a sense of **reverence.** "Reverence is one of man's answers to the presence of the mystery[10]." When we are caught up in wonder, our most natural and creative response is to hold that which is wonder-full in deep respect. We do not wish to penetrate its mystery, but rather desire its mystery to penetrate us.

The opposite of wonder is a presumptuous curiosity which seeks to control. One of the dynamics of existence seems to be that the attempted manipulation of the mysterious often brings about the destruction of the manipulator. This law is illustrated well in the Cheyenne story of "Fifty Young Men and a Turtle[11]." Fifty young men set off to go hunting. On their way they met a giant turtle. While recognizing that the turtle was a being of awe and mystery, one by one the warriors climbed onto the turtle's back and began trying to pry apart his shell with their spears to see how he was put together. Only the chief resisted this temptation. The young warriors soon found to their dismay that they were stuck to the turtle's back and that it was approaching a lake. The chief pleaded with the turtle, but it would or could not listen. As the turtle slipped into the water and his friends were about to be drowned, the chief made the following sorrowful observation to his friends: "I have done all I can do . . . Something wonderful was shown to you, and you did not respect it. Now you will be punished because you thought wrong in your hearts. I cannot change anything.[12]"

2. Reverence leads to a sense of **compassion.** A profound sense of compassion shines through some of the laws contained in the Hebrew Scriptures concerning the treatment of the land, of aliens, and of the poor (see, for example Leviticus 25:1-7, especially in the **New English Bible** verson). Agricultural land was allowed to rest — not for the technological reason so that it could continue producing in future years — but so that the people, and the land itself, could echo God's resting on the seventh "day" to enjoy the goodness of creation. Similarly, reverence and respect underlie the commandments concerning hospitality to strangers and provisions for the poor.

The notion of spiritual development is particularly important here. These examples of compassionate laws in the Hebrew Scriptures were not the result of a well-planned agricultural and social reform, but the spontaneous outward expressions of an inner attitude of reverence reflecting the wonder and mystery of God. G. K. Chesterton puts it this way:

> Morality did not begin by one man saying to another, "I will not hit you if you do not hit me;" there is no trace of such a transaction. There is a trace of both men having said, "We must not hit each other in the holy place." They gained their morality by guarding their religion . . . And only when they made a holy day for God did they find they had made a holiday for men.[13]

3. A sense or reverence and compassion for all life ignites **indignation** toward those who betray this trust. The power of this indignation comes through most forcefully in the prophetic tradition, a tradition to which Jesus of Nazareth stands in direct lineage. Jeremiah summarizes the power of God's word to smash human hypocrisy and pretentiousness:

> Is not my word like fire, says the Lord, like a hammer shattering rocks? (Jeremiah 23:29, NAB)

Abraham Joshua Heschel perceives a direct relationship between wonder, mystery, religion, and finally, ethics. In establishing the foundation for this relationship he states: "Religion is the result of what man does with his ultimate wonder, with the moments of awe, with the sense of mystery.[14]" He goes on to see the crucial question which God asks of each person as the challenge of where to go with this sense of wonder: "It is not a feeling for the mystery of living, or a sense of awe, wonder, or fear, which is the root of religion; but rather the question of **what to do** with the feeling for the mystery of living, what to do with awe, wonder, or fear.[15]" And it is precisely the process of grappling with this question which gives rise to ethical inquiry:

> In spite of our pride, in spite of our acquisitiveness, we are driven by an awareness that something is asked of us; that we are asked to wonder, to revere, to think and to live in a way that is compatible with the grandeur and mystery of living.
>
> What gives birth to religion is not intellectual curiosity but the fact and experience of our being asked.
>
> All that is left to us is a choice — to answer or to refuse to answer.[16]

4. Indignation has a double aspect. On the one hand, it can lead to violent retribution. On the other hand, within the context of wonder, reverence, and compassion for all life, it can lead to **forgiveness** and, finally, to **reconciliation**.

Prophetic indignation was never an end-in-itself. The hope behind the prophet's often harsh words was to provoke the people to repentance. Repentance, in turn, would elicit God's forgiveness, which would inspire forgiveness, and thus reconciliation, between person and person.

The above approach, while needed to provide some important input, tends to induce theological highs without necessarily touching the roots of experience. Theological input needs to be related to the actual life situations of the participants. This can be done through a discussion designed to encourage personal growth and communal sharing. The discussion starter which I use at this point can be found at the end of the paper.

The challenge of the third session is to encourage the persons in the program to explore wonder in terms of the life and person of Jesus. Such an exploration naturally lends itself to a discussion format similar to that used in the previous session. Wonder and its implications are re-searched in the light of the life, death, and resurrection of Jesus. I have found the sequence of wonder, reverence, compassion, forgiveness, and reconciliation to be particularly helpful here.

For example, the question "How do you think Jesus experienced wonder in his own life?" often leads to a fascinating discussion of Jesus' prayer life as reflected in the Gospels. We see in sharper relief Jesus' response to the wonder of God's call as the source of power for his ministry. We realize more clearly, for us in the Christian tradition, how Jesus fulfilled in his own life this observation by Abraham Joshua Heschel:

> A moment of awe is a moment of self-consecration. They who sense the wonder share in the wonder. They who keep holy the things that are holy shall themselves become holy.[17]

Returning to our initial description of wonder as radical amazement and abiding astonishment, we can begin to glimpse the source of Jesus' prayer life as the same stance of radical amazement and abiding astonishment to which we ourselves are called:

> The great turning points in religious history are based on the fact that again and ever again an individual and a group attached to him wonder and keep on wondering.[18]

Flowing from this profound sense of wonder which all of us can share with Jesus, we can see the reverence, the compassion, the indignation, the forgiveness, and the reconciliation of Jesus in some exciting new perspectives. Perhaps the most exciting of these is a deeper intuition concerning the mystery of the incarnation. We see that as Jesus' followers we are called to reflect precisely the same attitudes and actions that Jesus embodied in his own life. But at the same time the authority, the constancy, the simplicity, and the consistency of Jesus place our own short-comings in sharp contrast.

As one parishioner remarked concerning the schema of indignation-repentance-forgiveness-reconciliation: "It all sounds very nice, but how are we supposed to bring all this off in our own lives?" Interestingly, the same person observed later in the session that "I guess we just can't do these things alone."

Observations like this can spark in many a renewed understanding of the incarnation: the fact that we need Jesus **and each other** in order to ignite the implications of wonder as radical amazement and abiding astonishment in ourselves. Especially in the context of the Eucharist, we can see how Jesus' sacrifice of himself for us — and his continuing presence with us — was the only act of love strong enough to empower us to give ourselves for each other.

Not all Christian groups, of course, will come to the intuition that the Last Supper, and its completion in the crucifixion, is the high point of Jesus' attitude of self-giving wonder. For those who do, however, this is the perfect time for a spontaneous celebration of the Eucharist. In most traditions, the "words of institution" clearly bring out the fact that our God is a God of wonder. At this point a profound reversal takes place. We usually think of wonder as being the starting point of **our** reaching out to God. In the context of the Eucharist, however, we can see that, in the person of Jesus, **God** reaches out to us in wonder, a wonder which includes forgiveness and reconciliation:

> Father, it was not yesterday
>   that your care for us began,
>   but it was, as you say, in the beginning.
> In the beginning you spoke
>   and the world was made
>   and the story started
>   and the tale told.
> It was the tale of your great love.
> In the hearts of history's children,
>   the first men, our first fathers and mothers,
>   you planted your Word.
>   And they spun it out, spoke it,
>   haltingly, obscurely, but true.
> You chose among them Abraham
>   and the battered line of his sons and daughters.
>   They were to be great tellers of your tale.
>   Like us they were men of poor memory
>   and again and again they forgot.
> You sent them prophets and poets
>   burdened with your vision,
>   burning with your dream,
>   always saying this is so;
>   the yearnings of our hearts are messages from you.
> But there were other tales to tell,
>   other words to hear.
>   Our fathers were not faithful.
> And so it was you did the deed,
>   the completely unexpected one.
> You took the timeless hopes of men,
>   the search since once-upon-a-time
>   for light and one true Word of love.
> You took the ancient yearnings of men
>   and you made of them a man.[19]

Following this celebration, or, better yet, as an integral part of the celebration itself, reflections on the relationship between wonder and ritual can be explored. It is intriguing to watch a new understanding of ritual and sacrament unfold. Someone may pick up on the fact that a religious ritual is an outward expression of being grasped by inward wonder. Next may come the realization that a sacrament is God's wonder-full love toward persons expressed in a concrete way at a particular place and time. At this point someone will usually object that God loves us all the time anyway, so why make such a big deal about sacraments? — Which opens the door to the intuition that sacraments are really **celebrations** of God's love for us and our love for God. This insight, in turn, often inspires the observation that a healthy sense of wonder and mystery can ignite within us a sacramental attitude toward all of life — an attitude which is described most clearly in Jesus' own sense or reverence, compassion, indignation, forgiveness, and reconciliation.

I have found that this simple three session series (or intensive one day workshop) on wonder can literally work wonders in the attitudes of those attending. By encouraging the participants to affirm their own experiences of wonder, a whole new dimension of God's presence is opened to many persons. This dimension can be deepened through reflection and response.

Reflection can lead to the unfolding of some of the various implications of wonder, and to a response in terms of a personal ethic which is more profound, and a sense of celebration which is more joyful and spontaneous.

The following abbreviations refer to these versions of the Bible:
NAB — New American Bible
NEB — New English Bible

NOTES:

1. T.S. Eliot, "Burnt Norton," in *Four Quartets* (New York: Harcourt, Brace & World, 1943), p. 5.
2. Abraham J. Heschel, *Between God and Man: An Interpretation of Judaism,* selected, edited, and introduced by Fritz A. Rothschild (New York: Macmillan, 1965), p. 41.
3. Martin Buber, *Moses: The Revelation and the Covenant* (New York: Harper & Row, 1958), p. 75.
4. Heschel, p. 41.
5. Heschel, p. 42.
6. Heschel, p. 41.
7. Heschel, p. 41.
8. A full description of the sessions can be found at the end of this paper.
9. A listing of recommended resources is included in the complete description of the sessions.
10. Heschel, p. 54.
11. In the book *American Indian Mythology* by Alice Marriott and Carol K. Rachlin (New York: Crowell, 1968), pp. 41-45.
12. *American Indian Mythology,* p. 44.
13. G.K. Chesterton, *Orthodoxy* (Garden City, New York: Doubleday, 1959), p. 68.
14. Heschel, p. 60.
15. Heschel, p. 60.
16. Heschel, pp. 60-61.
17. Heschel, p. 54.
18. Buber, p. 75.
19. James Carroll, *Wonder and Worship* (New York: Newman, 1970), pp. 140-141.

A Project in Fullness of Learning Eucharist

By SUSAN BELL
Alexandria, Va.

"This group shared all the things that mean the life of the church to us — my experience has been a 180 degree turn in my attitude toward Eucharist — it should be a celebration, a joyous occasion — I now feel a oneness with this group — it was my first experience trying to discover what Eucharist is all about — we celebrate Christ's life — a stunningly appropriate way of acting out our belief that Christ is the one who nourishes our spirits."

These comments were shared with the congregation by members of a leadership team after a ten week study of Eucharist. This leadership group of twelve adults met weekly exploring the meaning of Eucharist and planning a six week study unit on Eucharist for the church school. This unit fit within the existing church school structure, an open classroom for first graders through adults. An important aspect of this project was that during the six week unit, Eucharist was discussed within the other ongoing church groups (youth and women) and provided the sermon topics. This gave added dimension to the task of the leadership team, for we had the opportunity to provide an experience of growth in Eucharist life for the entire congregation, rather than creating an "in group" with its own special understanding. We appreciated this more during our study as we came to realize that the meaningful world of Eucharist comes from and is nurtured within the total corporate life.

I structured the ten sessions with the leadership team to provide a full learning experience, one that would include four major contents. The first of these is belonging. All learning is possibly first a new belonging, meaning that a person is not open to change, to becoming different, until he feels in his deepest being that he belongs to a group. Learning within a Christian framework requires that we start with the community of believers, for faith develops and is communicated within a group of people out of their history, by interaction with each other, and in relation to the events of their lives. The nature and quality of the group life was important, for the inner world and experience of others has the greatest power to awaken each of us and let us grow. The group then needed to be a place:

> where each felt free to open himself and be drawn into communion,
> where we became aware of one another as presence, knowing each other as subjects, sensing one another's mystery and depth,
> where we shared meaningful information and the enlargement of experiences,
> and where meanings matured from deep feelings and experiencing.

Identifying and expanding perceptions and images constitute a second part of a full learning experience. Much time was spent sharing our perceptions of Eucharist — the flow of feeling and significance. Eucharist depends, however, upon the perception of God as a living reality present in concrete encounters. It is a qualitatively different experience for those who see it as the opportunity for the in-breaking of the love and power of God rather than as a remembrance.

The third content of learning is experience. This project focused on celebrating Eucharist frequently within the group. I hoped these celebrations would not be isolated events, but that Eucharist would begin to be seen as one of the great organizing experiences of Christian life and faith, in which the meaning of life is made powerfully present.

Meanings, the meaningful world present in Eucharist, is the fourth content of a full learning experience. Meanings arise from events and experiences as organizing centers, revealing and explaining segments of life. Many Christians bring from Eucharist only an accumulation of vague feelings that are never nurtured into full meanings or significant symbol. Through regular sharing of Eucharist I hoped real meanings would mature within the group, and that these meanings would interpret and enrich other experiences.

The church where I led this study of Eucharist is a small Methodist church in Alexandria, Virginia. Eucharist was celebrated no more than three or four times a year. The congregation went in small groups to the altar rail, where each person received a wafer that was dipped into a common cup. The service was simple, with little congregational participation other than receiving the elements. The tone was solemn and contemplative, resulting in a personal, individual experience.

As we began our study these were some initial perceptions of Eucharist shared by members of this congregation:

> Many felt Eucharist centered solely on the events of the Last Supper and Jesus' death; that Eucharist should be a sober remembrance of that event, the most appropriate time being Maundy Thursday.
>
> The words "body" and "blood" caused some discomfort.
>
> The emotional tone was described as "draining" and "depressing."
>
> More frequent Eucharist was not desirable — the meaning was so profound that celebrating more often would detract from the "specialness" of it.
>
> One man in the leadership group did not participate in Eucharist because he felt he had an inadequate understanding of its meaning.

Given the infrequent celebration and the perceptions of many in this congregation, I saw three major possibilities for our study of Eucharist. The primary one was to expand our celebration from a commemoration to an encounter — to experience the present power of Christ in our midst and in the world. In J. T. Robinson's words, "when we come to the Eucharist we come not simply to a representation of something that has happened . . . we come to be present at — and at the same time to present, to transmit to the world — something that is happening." Here the redeeming act of Christ is made operative in the present, as the Christian community offers itself to be transformed and renewed. The focus shifts from the presence of Christ being bound up with the elements to being alive in the gathered community. And finally, the tone moves from solemn remembering to expectancy and celebration.

A second possibility for the unit involved our participation as Body of Christ, not as isolated individuals. In I Corinthians 10:17 Paul says, "Because there is one loaf, we who are many are one body, for we all partake of the same loaf." For Paul, the concept of the Body of Christ was represented not only by the bread and wine, but also by the community of believers. The small group setting more easily evidences the communal aspect — not that we are all simply doing it at the same time, but that we share a special relationship with one another as members of Christ's Body.

A final possiblity was to sense that we gather in Eucharist not only to celebrate our life together, but to become Christ's instrument in the world. The task of the church is to "present to the world — or rather let Christ present through us — the drama, the finished act of its redemption."

The first two sessions of the leadership group created a sense of community and began our sharing our understanding of Eucharist. At our first session I asked group members to prepare a personal timeline, graphing along a horizontal line the events of their lives and how they saw them now. After taking about twenty minutes to complete them we shared with one another for about two hours.

This was one of our most valuable experiences together, though at the time several people questioned what this had to do with Eucharist. Within a setting of respect, humor, and at points real empathy, we simply enjoyed learning about each other, and especially talking about ourselves to a somewhat captive audience. Often as the weeks passed something from the timelines would be remembered or referred to, whether the glory of being a high school basketball star that several men shared or the difficulty of coping with terminal illness in the family.

At another level, however, this first session spoke directly to the Eucharist experience. As our perceptions of each other took on dimension and fullness, the foundation was laid for sharing in a deeper and more personal way. Our sense of belonging was strengthened. We also began to relate the Eucharist to our own concrete experiencing and the events of our lives. Often Eucharist seems to have little contact with the "stuff and muck" of the world. Rather than bringing this world into the power and presence of Christ, it seems to create an artificial world of its own, a world of sacred things over against the secular. The Eucharist should instead speak to a deeper immersion in spirited, personal existence. It was important as we celebrated together to make contact with the lives of the people present.

The timelines also clarified what has become for me the over-arching concept of Eucharist, which is presence — Christ's presence with us, in our lives, in the world, symbolized in the Eucharist, and our real presence with one another. As we attempt to get away from asking the wrong question — how is Christ present in the elements, the concept of personal presence, the way one person is and remains present to another, even when physically absent, is a helpful one. Personal presence is no less mysterious, and no more objectifiable, than the personal presence of any one individual to another. It requires a genuine mutuality, a free self-communication, and a spiritual openness. This personal communication occurs when one person freely reveals himself, and another receives that self-revelation in an atmosphere of faith and trust. It may well take place when one person is physically present to another, but the reality is far greater than mere physical presence.

In later sessions, as we discussed the meaning of Eucharist, we looked back to our first session and how our sharing had made us personally present to one another. One woman expressed it: "I carry this group around with me all week. I think about who you are, what you've shared with us, and some thing you said on Tuesday night strikes me fresh Thursday morning. You are real people to me." In a group that has made some beginnings at being personally present to one another, the idea of Christ's presence being a personal, non-objectifiable presence beings to come into focus.

A continuing part of our study unit was sharing our perceptions of Eucharist. For our second session each person was asked to prepare in advance a paper on the flow of feeling experienced during Eucharist, and the meaning of what was going on. Other groups in the church participated in this, too. We discovered during these discussions, along with the initial perceptions mentioned earlier, a concern with the mechanics, and a general feeling within our leadership team that Eucharist was a positive spiritual experience, but without much specific meaning or contact with real life. Two particular questions emerged during this sharing which needed to be pursued within the church beyond the scope of this unit. One was how this congregation understood and experienced the presence of Christ, for this is the basic theological foundation of the Eucharist. A second question was how much of our religious life can be included within the meaning of Eucharist. If it is about celebrating, belonging, peace, sharing a meal, love, and transforming the world, have we so diffused the original meaning that Eucharist as a celebration is simply anything we want to make of it? Yet had we not begun with, and continued to explore our perceptions, and the real concerns and questions that emerged from them, I doubt we would have been able to arrive at meanings which were, or became, truly expressive of our congregation.

Having shared something of ourselves and our understanding of Eucharist in the first two sessions, the remaining meetings with the leadership team focused on providing experiences that would expand our understanding and from which new meanings would emerge and grow. Material was presented on the Biblical background, the symbolism of the Passover and Jewish religious meals, and the Eucharist practices in the early church. We saw and discussed a film on the life themes of Eucharist — the elemental human experiences (new life, nourishment, acceptance, fellowship) that Eucharist draws upon for its power as a symbol. Twice our group met with members of a neighboring Catholic church for discussion and an agape meal. But while these experiences expanded our information, it was the celebration of Eucharist itself from which real meanings came alive and matured within the group.

With the exception of the first night, the planning group celebrated together at almost every session. Often we met in homes, and for many it was the first experience of Eucharist outside the church. Bread and wine were usually provided by the host. Ordinary dishes were often used, and preparing the table, pouring the wine, became a part of our service. We used several different liturgies, minimizing the role of the minister to make it as truly as possible the action of the people present. Our final service used no words, letting the action alone carry the meaning.

Much of the meaning came through for us as we began to take seriously the sign value of the action of Eucharist — an action of multi-sensory richness and diversity that conveys the meaning of the sacrament as well as presents the pattern of Christian life. In the offering, bread and wine represent our lives: bread, our need for physical nourishment, the complexity of life, and our inter-relatedness — wine, the ambiguity of life, its joy and sorrow. These become symbols of the offering of ourselves that takes place each time we celebrate. The sign value of real bread, the basic food of life, rather than a tasteless wafer, connects with the symbolism of a shared fellowship meal. Only a common loaf, which really needs to be broken for distribution, expresses the meaning of the fraction, that the life of God can be given and shared only if it is broken — that those who celebrate the Eucharist are bound with Christ in the same self-sacrifice — the willingness to become bearers of new life. The sign value of the sharing, when people serve and speak the words to one another, points to the gathering of Christ's people rather than a private devotion. Primarily the growth of new meanings came for us as we tried to make more explicit the action of the Eucharist and relate this action to our own lives. I would summarize these meanings as follows:

> Celebration, the joyful affirmation of Christian life, is the appropriate mood for the gathering of Christ's people in Eucharist.
>
> Eucharist draws its power as a symbol from the basic experiences of human life. It does not demand our entering a special realm of sacred things.
>
> Eucharist is an action of the community, as well as an individual experience.
>
> An underlying unity of meaning in the Eucharist crosses denominational lines.
>
> Eucharist has an outward thrust — as we are formed into Christ's Body to carry on the renewing and transforming in the world.
>
> Christ's presence with us, and our presence with one another, can be understood in terms of personal presence.
>
> We became more aware of our own perceptions of Eucharist, and how to nurture growth rather than try to impose meanings on a group.

One final aspect of this project is the image of ministry involved in this kind of a group. A part of this ministry is to nurture the self-awareness and self-actualization of the persons in the group, "helping to bring to birth the thought, feeling, new creation that is a faint stirring within them." But another and equally important ministry, as the leader, is sharing yourself at appropriate moments — the truth, the offering of life that you affirm. I learned through this project that most people are only mildly interested in theology or Biblical history as information. What does seem to stir thought and invite response is an affirmation — where this "information" comes alive for me — and the sharing of experiences together in which the meanings of life are clarified and take on significant form.

Looking back on this project two aspects of our sharing and learning about Eucharist become clear. One is that the Eucharist experience itself is the most powerful conveyor of the meanings of this symbol, and that through sharing Eucharist regularly, within a group that in some sense becomes a Eucharist community, its meanings mature and grow. Simply to discuss it does not result in the co-creation of meanings which everyone can in some sense affirm. The climax of the leadership group's experience was when the man who had previously stepped back from the circle as we shared the bread and wine joined in the final celebration. It said to us that along with sharing ideas and information, we had created something new together of which we all were a part.

A second conclusion is that Eucharist cannot be explored in isolation from the total life of the church. Genuine Eucharist celebration is rooted in the center of the church's life — its worship life, its theological foundations, and its life as a community. While the meanings which have surrounded Eucharist through the centuries, as well as the Biblical background, are necessary for centering this event, no one can tell a congregation all that Eucharist means. The meanings of this celebration must result from a co-creation that is nourished by every aspect of the church's life. A new sensing of the richness and depth of Eucharist must relate powerfully to life experiences, matured into meanings, so that Eucharist celebration is truly one that "with impact sets forth the life world of the people present."

Images
Containing Futures

I APPRECIATIVE MIND

Life is too short not to see possibilities, hearingly listen to our imagination and our appreciations.
>Never to hear the big bells ringing
>Never to walk into a region where one's head is bathed in clouds of freshness
>Never to escape the drivenness of time...and coping...and the tenseness toward winning.
>Never to allow the internal milieu its chance to do its growing
>Never to honk anticipatory resoluteness
>Never to exult in shouting "nevertheless" to monstrous lies and brutalities
>Never to migrate resoundingly in a golden V down ancestral trails to originating home
>Never to sing with heart and mind and strength the songs we want to utter
>Never to listen to Inner Speech...where Mysteries of transformation and creation constantly want to go on

II CONSUMMATORY MIND

1

"This work of my hands expresses something that's important to me.
>That line of movement is the quick of my energy. I felt very intensely when I did that.
>There's a melody line in the work...carrying on a conversation with a foundational tune coming from roots of life in deep earth.
>What I have done is not neutral gray, but participates in the sky blue-green of spring...in which there is an oak tree. In it are spots of light and blocks of shadow. But a luminescence comes thru it all that's my spirit.
>My thrust to take on significant form, my mind that can turn even darkness into a design of meaning, my spirit that pulses through a disciplined body...has gone on a trail, put together and culminated a meaning.
>I came through. At some point in the work, pain and struggle were transformed into power...I stated my hunch. I fought for a vision of something better becoming real. I played the part of **human being**. I now know better where the battles are, and the strategies to be developed."

I am creation
>clear, intense, fascinating form
>active, potent, desirable.

2

"I may not be much, but the cause I serve is tremendous.
I'm matching myself to human need. This particular enterprise is necessary...and now is the time.
This experiment in existence is in the direction of humankindness. It's worth the best I can give it. I **mean** it. I mean it in this **particular** way.

Through many years, people of dimensions have been working in this enterprise. Developing it. There's quite a lore about it — anecdotes, stories, snatches of language, that form and power it. All that is present right now.

The labor of my hands and mind, the fidelity of my heart...helps create this which I love. It is something "whom to serve is perfect freedom.""

3

"In what we just did, the people were members one of another."

There are some people in this world that will not desert me, or bad-mouth me. They were there when I desperately needed help. I didn't have to keep looking over my shoulder to see if someone was sneaking up on me. They are not triflers, nor traitors.

One or two are especially knowledgeable. If you're stuck they have the words and acts that straighten out the enterprise and once more it moves.

They are fellow craftsmen...who know workmanship.

Yes, they are earthen vessels. Often fragile...their foundations sliding around. Intermittently a Truth. Caught. Trapped in a fate and there seems no way out.

But we have our "remember when?"

Such are the people with whom I am working.

As for people in general...
"There are men who can't be bought"
"The fireborn do not fear the fire"
"Children's laughter is right"
"The People...yes."
"A habitation of God thru the spirit."

**Images
Containing Futures**

IV
"The Lords Free People"
PSYCHOHISTORY

Psychohistory is one person's contribution to the inventing of spiritual Man.
They lived in an intense moment of person-making
   an insurgent survivor
      became "the voice meaning it"
         Fashioning out of his heritage
         and his own life
         the new humanness
         that time in history had to bring off.
Born in a predawn
   He developed rather than crawled
   thru history
He came through
   A tough-textured developmental human
   In a world on the move.
     "What does not kill me
     strengthens me."

2

He came out in integrity
   able to re-mean the world
   which was too much for many people.
In spite of defeats and suffering
   Life still had valences and consummations
He transformed
   Found a theme and a story
   which made him a human dignity

3

The consummation of psychohistory is this —
   "And Moses died, not having received the promises
   But he saw the Promised Land."

4

Psychohistory concentrates on a person's battles for meaning
  rather than upon psychological determinisms
More upon synthesis and what they found to go with
  than upon a diagnosis of what was wrong.
We do psychohistory
  for the purpose of learning positively
    from the people we study
What we are trying to learn
  is not how to win
    but how to be magnificently human.

Images Containing Futures

ARCHETYPE

Far into the never-ceasing night that attempts to destroy humankind, the memory of archetypes such as John Wycliff, will enable some authentics to utter a "nevertheless," and bring sources of freedom that cannot be extinguished.
In a world of domination by principalities and powers they will be a voice and a courage which threat and loneness cannot disintegrate.
> Their lives will assert that each person is a human dignity, endowed with potencies for being human that cannot be violated or profaned... with impunity.
> They will have direct access to documents which tell this secret of history-making. And they will make that mythhistory widely available in forms that all can understand.

And God's yeomen with the long bows will once again bring down the knights and ladies of arrogance and torture and monstrous stupidities.
> And the Lord's free people shall make one more journey toward the land where they shall be like a tree planted by the rivers of water.

Let the image of John Wycliffe be a frame in your mind's eye with which to discern your vocation on earth.

AMEN AND AMEN

Images Containing Futures

CHRIST THE TRANSFORMER
AS A MODE OF BEING IN THE WORLD

> "Christ takes form in a band of persons
> Christ takes form in the midst of the world."
>   (Bonhoeffer)

Bonhoeffer's phrase "the form of Christ" suggests that Christ is not just the events and teachings of the life of Jesus of Nazareth...**Christ is a mode of**

being-in-the-world by a personal center. *A personal center* **that is also an intersubjectivity** *now taking form in a body of persons.*

2

Christ is a verb, not a noun. Or perhaps more accurately, a verb-noun.

Christ is originative personal energy taking into itself what is going on and transmuting it into new possibility. A transforming variable that interposes itself between the present and a mere repetition of what now is.

So fundamentally a Christian is expressive spontaneity — a love and creativeness and hilaritas* that, in each particular situation of life, takes into itself the joy and agony, the good and evil, of that situation, and is not overcome by it. But in conjunction with others, transforms it into new possibility which it offers to God and man.

***Hilaritas** — "a confidence in their work, a certain kind of baldness and defiance of the world and popular opinion, a steadfast certainty that what they are doing will benefit the world even tho it does not approve, a magnificent self-awareness (a certain kind of cheerfulness)." — Bonhoeffer "Letters and Papers from Prison" p. 142.

Christ is an incarnation of God's urge to become manifest. To take on significant form. Particularly in difficult situations.

3

What is the secret of this mode? Participation at the same time in both God's struggle **and** *in the workings of a very ambiguous — and somewhat functionally autonomous world.*

The events about us of creation and destruction, of agony and triumph, of meaningfulness and meaninglessness...the personal realities with whom we are living...are received, digested, transformed into **possibility-on-its-way-to-becoming.** *Working in and with the situation, we enlist the components of that particular area of life to share in bringing off outcomes.*

4

This is not just non-violent resistance. This is rather a resolute becoming-something-different. And going thru a cross event if necessary.

> *For the point of the cross is not that we suffer. But that we sensitively feel the agony and struggle of our fellow man and willingly enter into a situation we could avoid if we wanted a safe and pleasurable life.*

> *And instead of being overcome by evil, we exist as this transforming, innovating consciousness and person. Even though we may not succeed in the immediate time and situation.*

Such existence is that which creates us and a society of persons. That which, above all, we cannot become estranged from or cease to participate in. For Christ is an immediacy. He is not an ideal, but a working originative energy...to participate in, and again and again celebratively hold dialogue with.

The **form** *of Christ must* **take form** *within us. And within a corporateness. Only with this can we stand...in the turmoil, tension, difficulties of a world becoming more and different than it now is."*

An Enterprise: The Consciousness of a People

By TOM CUNNINGHAM
Methodist Church
S. Africa

In a country where controversy reigns over an apartheid policy which affects a people's culture and creates inherent conflict with violence already almost part of our way of life, not many opportunities are offered for ministers of different races to hear each other or grow together in a common enterprise. The Post Ordination Training Course of the Methodist Church attempts to provide this for ordained ministers in South Africa. The setting is Johannesburg or Durban. In Johannesburg special permission has to be obtained from Government sources for Blacks to stay at the Conference centre for the period of 10 days.

Two such Courses are held each year. At the most recent Course one participant (a white) wrote these words in his "My Story of the Course":

"I volunteered to come on the Course **reluctantly** because: both spiritual and physical health was at a low ebb and I could not see purpose in attending such a Course — and living in close confinement with other ministers over a period of ten days, each determined to impress the others with a sense of his own self-importance.

But seeing I was on this Course, I was determined to try and get **something** out of it, to see if there was any chance of sorting out some of my personal problems....to see where I stood in relation to:
    Myself -
      my brethren
        and my ministry as a whole.

And of course - to try and find out if there was any use in continuing in the ministry in our present South African situation - TO KNOW WHERE I STAND."

A NEED TO BECOME MANIFEST, TO EXIST

As I reflect on some of the experiences in these Courses there is an existence in each of the ministers struggling to get out. To be born again. To have something to live for, and maybe, to die for. In some it seems like an inner fire, perhaps a little dampened, but waiting to be rekindled so that its flames can dance again with a burning desire to reach out, take hold of, and delight in, the promises of life.

Ernest Baartman, a Black theologian, and with me, co-facilitator of the Course, says: "There is something distinctive happening here. The Black men in our Courses have discovered a being swept into a new understanding of what it means to be a person." This certainly became evident during the last Course. I felt some excitement when the men opened themselves to each other. Len, a white, said: "I believe that when you Blacks take over you will let in communists, and you will be worse off."

The Black delegates laughed when he said this. I watched keenly waiting to see the response, because, I am always aware that on this Course sooner or later these issues need to surface, and I am not always sure how the men will deal with them. The laughter of the Blacks was not cynical nor was it in disgust. It came to me more as that of men who had found a new confidence in themselves and a deep concern for the one who had completely misunderstood them.

One Black said: "You can call us nationalists if you want to — just as you Whites are nationalists. But is is a mistake to call us communists."
Another joined in: "When I look at communism, I see three things: you cannot go where you like, You cannot own property, you cannot vote for whom you like. And then I look at our situation as Blacks, and see no difference!"

Yet another: "Come with me to the townships, see the children there, how poor they look, see the unsmiling mothers, see the drabness, and then come tell me if we could be worse off."

So in the emerging development of this group there was a struggle to become manifest. To become known is contrasted with the urge to remain hidden so that the duplicities, the naive nuances and fears, are kept submerged.

This enterprise like several before it begins with opportunities for community building. Helping participants to find each other and discover people who care for each other and something together.

EXPLORING THROUGH LIFE REFLECTIONS

Some of the most vivid experiencings occur when we have introduced a method of theologising which we call "life Reflections". We try to help each other explore experiences, retaste them, and discover the potential for new possibilities that God is giving us. We follow the pattern of
SELF REVELATION
UNDERSTANDING
MEANING

Each of these are disciplined steps, enabling us to explore in as much depth as possible what is occuring in our life and ministry, and what meanings there are for us. This way we begin living creatively, with potentialities for being exploding within and around us.

We usually ask participants to describe events or experiences which are not too distant in the past. Ron, however, wanted to deal with an experience which had been worrying him for 18 years and which he felt was blocking his life at this moment. His colleagues on the Course struggled with him in his ordeal for two hours. There were no easy answers and in the end one of the men asked if we could all pray together with Ron. All fell onto knees. A rug was placed in the middle of the floor for Ron. One Black minister placed his hands on Ron's head, another held his hands, and a third Black minister stood next to him. The rest of us knelt in the form of a circle. In that formation we prayed together. I think it was the first time that Ron had experienced such close contact with his Black colleagues. It is not always that Blacks are free to minister to Whites, and the impact was quite dramatic.

LEARNING THROUGH SIGNIFICANT PEOPLE

Further learning in this group comes about through significant resource people whom we bring into the Course. George Irvine and Paul Welsh help us look at preaching and counseling. "Preaching is the offering of the Good News," they tell us, "rather than the easier way of telling people what they ought to do." Paul emphasizes "Good News" to the point of saying "no law preaching at all." George, on the other hand, says: "reverse what is usually done in Methodist preaching, and, preach Good News ninety-percent, and law only ten percent if you have to." Bob's response was: "Yes, I would like to agree, but how do we help people to see the need for justice, love and mercy, and point out the responsibilities of Christians in our Society, when all we do is preach 'good news'?

I felt that we needed a shift in focus. I always remember how Ernest so often described his or some other situation in the lives of Black people. He did it with such intense feeling, understanding, and from the point of view of a sufferer, that I was always pricked in conscience and felt uncomfortable, realizing that I, a White, was the oppressor. This led me to say: "I believe that identifying with those who suffer, or are persecuted, or oppressed, isn't done by preaching law at guilty people. It is rather standing with those who are suffering and describing with intensity and feeling their position. In other words, **agonising** with the sufferer." This way is not preaching **at** people, but it is lifting up pieces of real life in such a way that people are themselves able to identify with suffering. When that is done we are ready to hear 'good news' of who the Christ is in such situations, so that we ourselves might become part of the truth, and be good news for others. In this descriptive method, that is, agonising in the situation, we do not need to tell people by means of law preaching, what to do, people will know what they must do.

When Brian Brown came to our Course from the Christian Institute (a prophetic Christian movement in South Africa), he helped us look at what is so neglected in our style as ministers, the prophetic. Brian came across to me as a man who has earned his rigtht to be numberd among those of the prophetic tradition. He is uncompromising in his stand for justice and at the same time spreads such warmth and love that his message is unmistakable.

"Why do we as ministers back away from a prophetic style of ministry?" he asks. "Or at least include the prophetic with the priestly role?" Ted (White) said: "For me the reason is that if you speak out you are likely to be intimidated by members of the congregation. In fact one is likely to end up in gaol." This opened up the discussion and we began to realize that from the White side we do not only fear the rule of the Black man, but also the White power structure. And for this reason we prefer to go along with the tide. There was no doubt about it - the Blacks present were disgusted at this White standpoint. Gordon said: "Whites have never had occasion to suffer, they are oppressors. Are you not willing to lead with your chin. We all suffer as a body, because when one part of the suffers the whole body needs suffer with it."

Another Black: "We don't have any choice we have to take a stand - if we don't we become irrelevant, and that means we stand a greater chance of being killed."

"It is not merely an ideal for which we are standing, its simply that if we don't move towards a just society we will die."

Another Black spelled out the reality even more starkly: "Our presence with you is detrimental. We find ourselves in a reconciliatory role and this is unacceptable to many people. It is unacceptable to the power structures, and is is also unacceptable to many Blacks in the country. We are in the middle. This is the cost of our presence with you."

We Whites began to understand why Blacks are so disgusted when we fail to take significant stands and to be prepared to suffer for the sake of truth. Brian Brown told of his own experience: "I recall being asked by an anxious leader of a Church to which I had been invited whether it was my intention to "preach politics". To his initial relief I replied, no, for I was not inclined to push any one political viewpoint or policy. There is quite enough of this in our South African pulpits, where an apartheid policy has long been presented to the faithful. I then asked my friend if he would expect me to be silent on issues of justice and compromise myself in prophetic proclamation concerning God's demands? I would preach prophetically, not politically, and he got the message if not satisfaction."

MYTH OF A PEOPLE

In the context of our situtation we think of a people who for many years toiled and laboured for the Egyptian overlords. They were told by their masters where to work, where they may sleep, and with whom, where they may go, and may not go. Through this they developed a slave mentality, a slave culture. In return for their obedience they were tolerated and rewarded in kind. But one day there came a man of their own kin who exhorted them to stand up, become manifest, to come away from the masters and exist a new people. So they begged their masters to let them be free. The overlords, however, would not let this happen. Stronger measures were used to persuade them and eventually they consented, though even at the last moment an attempt was made to prevent the slaves from going free. The people began their journey to become a new community. They soon discovered the difference. As they wandered in the desert they found themselves to be no longer slaves but their own masters.

It takes a little time for their new consciousness to shake all the way down their system, and to realize they are no longer the same people. For you can't live like a slave when you do not have overlords. There is no master to whom you run along for an order, to be told what to do, to be given the next meal ticket. You have to do it yourselves. A whole new way of living, a new consciousness has to be worked out. Its another culture emerging.

Meanwhile, what happens to the overlords? They suddenly find they have no slaves, no servants. And the fact that they have to do the hard work from now on is not the most difficult thing - they could, and did, accommodate that problem. The real problem was their culture. How do you live without having servants who are part of the structure of your life, who are an extension of your bodies, who are part of the meaning of your life? A culture was being lost, and a new culture needed to emerge to make sense of what was happening.

Meanwhile the wanderers in the desert could not easily accept their cultural change and often wanted to return to their former masters. Nevertheless they pressed on until the new culture began to emerge. It was represented in the event at Mt. Sinai in the form of the Ten Commandments. But even at that moment, when the old culture was dying and a new had not yet been born, there seems to be a vacuum. In that moment people looked for new masters and found them in false creations which do not give hope, only immediate release. New culture is not a switch on with computerised immediacy. It is a growing that comes from first hand experiencing and living. Nevertheless as they formed their covenants their new and distinctive culture was being shaped and a new people were being born.

That could not be the ending. For the day culture making stopped, a people dies. When a people ceases to discover the power of new meanings to live out of, they cease to be. So it is that in our enterprise we encourage participants to ask the deep down question:

    WHAT MEANINGS
    CAN SO EXIST ME
    THAT I CAN BELIEVE
    AND BE BORN AGAIN?

A South African Black Classroom

JUNE N. PYM
S. Africa

LIVED MOMENT

Sixty students sit in my classroom with their heads bowed over writing material, seemingly engrossed in pre-final examinations. Through the dirty, sometimes shattered window panes, the urban ghetto throbs — a conglomeration of smoke and the noise of traffic; and yet the stillness in the classroom pervades the whole. There is a sense of calm ... a short soft breath amidst the general rasping rhythm.

The sanctity is disturbed by a far off droning sound; students in the classroom shuffle restlessly; the hum increases, finally breaking into the silence. A student stands to look out the window and shouts with jubilation ... "They've come!" Within seconds, students from neighboring schools have walked into the classroom and are inviting others to join them on a protest march to the city ... a protest against the inferior education to which they as Black people are subjected. The students vacilate between forthrightness and fear — they are aware of the possible consequences of such action, but are also awed by the powerful sense of possibility in sharing such an action and vision together. All too quickly examination papers lie strewn pathetically across the empty room. The students have walked out, to participate in the events of a new and what will be, horrifying existential experience.

When the new day dawns, those students return ... but they are changed. Their march was responded to with overwhelming violence, but they have also shared in the first tastes of unifying their vision with others. Vanessa, previously a giggly girl and fairly dulled-to-the world around her, now stands before her fellow students powerfully addressing and critiquing their action, their points of irresponsibility, their need to reflect, to replan their direction and vision. Students eagerly respond, question. This event and metamorphosis continues to evolve and so unfold a new and yet unknown chapter in this land.

PHENOMENOLOGIZING

A sense of acquiescence and seeming calm pervades the classroom as students begin their pre-final examinations. A shout and a call to march into the city breaks the pattern; these students are now no longer a bunch of jabbering people either passively waiting to absorb what they are 'fed' or wildly, desperately and without direction, trying to break the fetters. They are a serious group of 16 year olds who have experienced something intensely and are beginning to realize and **take charge of their own limits** and **their responsibility to one another**. But mostly there is a strong sense of **being in something together**. The students had contended not just against the present, but **for** the oncoming future.

THEOLOGIZING

This event lifts up that education enterprise **standing within events,** participating from the **in**-side so as to comprehend the processes and structures of whatever life one is deeply engaged in, can be generative of culture, and of Spirit. This understanding of and participation in concrete instances rather than broad generalities, awakens and channels new energies, making possible much more powerful "worlding" of life-space. Correspondingly, this increases the capacities of students involvement and taking charge of his or her own life. This is particularly important in the light of a history of severe bondage that has allowed little opportunity to "take charge".

The event also implies clearly the educational value of an experience that is **within the realm of the students world** i.e. taking seriously the particularity of the political, social, personal and physical environment of which the student is a part.

As one who teaches, I am to be involved in putting aside mere abstraction and fragmentation that might prove or fit into previous moulds and patterns; it involves working from a basis of lived events that are intrinsically valued and not merely a means to an end.

In this event, vividly so, is also the power of **mutuality.** So we need an education program that affords the opportunity for joint, shared enterprises, reporting to each other what sort of stirrings and learnings welled up here, and thus a growing sense of responsibility with and for each other. This is particularly important in a classroom where competitiveness and the fear of failing are predominant dynamics ... any interchange often being seen as a threat to the possible recognition of the individual.

The whole event was not just a "happening", sporadic and unrelated. It was complex, dense, and multi-faceted. It takes **time and sensitive processing** to discover its own peculiar texture, to birth the new possibility in it. Within it, not yet fully incarnated into a vision, is a **potential** ... **a power to shape** one's history, a new destiny.

Towards Spirited Existence In English-speaking South African Churches

BY JAMES ROGIERS COCHRANE
S. Africa

There is truth in the claim that the English-speaking churches of South Africa are sleeping through a revolution. Black dis-affection and white cynicism and indifference with respect to the pronounciations of these churches is increasingly evident.[1] To a large extent this is a reflection of our failure to witness to the gospel. The failure of the churches though, is directly related to the failures of English-speaking South Africa itself. So let us begin there.[2]

"We must somehow take a wider view, look at the whole landscape, really see it, and describe what's going on here. Then we can at least wail the right question into the swaddling band of darkness, or, if it comes to that, choir the proper praise."[3]

I.

At one point during the recent urban unrest in South Africa, when, in Cape Town, the number of shot and killed blacks was rising rapidly and it became dangerous to travel certain highways for fear of being stoned by angry people, I decided to seek the feelings and reactions of the second-year university students I was teaching. Almost all are so-called English-speaking South Africans. Almost all have a measure of sympathy for black South Africans. I waited for their comments.

— "I fear for my future here!"
— "It doesn't matter **what** you think - you're only another white to them."
— "I'm buying a gun, because if I get caught in a crowd, it's my life against their's."
— "I'm not black, and I'm not Afrikaner; I just cannot see any role for me."
— "I'm finishing my degree and getting out of here."

II.

In these statements, one hears the broad themes of a contemporary psyche. Immediately apparent are strong elements of defensiveness; of insecurity; of self-protection; of confusion; and of escape. Certainly there is nothing generative of culture here, nor any sense that positive, affirmative proposals may emerge. In fact, self-insignificance and apparent powerlessness prevail. These I believe are the hallmarks of a deep and crippling neurosis in white English-speaking South Africa. It is thus not surprising that 'fear of the future' undermines present possibilities, and the roots thereof lie in our lack of understanding of ourselves in relation to our past. As Ross Snyder might put it, there is little of a past-present-future that is filled with destiny.

III.

Carl Jung has argued persuasively for the need in human beings of what I will call an intergrative Mythos - a set of symbols, rituals, paradigms, narratives, and assertions which unite the conscious and the unconscious, the phenomenal and the mysterious, the profane and the sacred, and which serve to orient and inform, explain and articulate human existence. Ross Snyder has pointed to the same need in calling the church to a "ministry of meanings". In both Jung and Snyder is the clear implication that human broken-ness or neurosis has to do with the lack or the loss, of mythos, or of an orb of meanings.[4] In a deep sense this is a loss of self. We are cast adrift in time, unable to comprehend our past, or influence our present, or welcome the future. It is precisely this kind of loss or lack and its manifestation in neurosis, that seems to characterize a large chunk of white English-speaking South Africa today. Why should this be so? There are many reasons. In order to seek clues towards generating new spirit, we will try here to examine the breakdown in the Ecology of Spirit.

THE HISTORICAL DILEMMA

In South Africa it is the Afrikaner puritans who are counterparts to the first white American settlers in New England.[5] They were the revolutionaries and rebels. In contrast, the first major group of English-speaking settlers, arriving at the Eastern Cape in 1820, were brought in under colonial policy to stabilize the frontier region where black and white had already clashed. The lure was economic, the intent stabilization. The people who arrived then, and the later settlers who cashed in on the diamond and gold discoveries in Kimberley and on the Reef in the second half of the Nineteenth Century, were enjoying the fruits of a widely extended British Empire motivated by the commitment and vision of the Victorian dream.[6] Together with this milieu went the individualism growing out of the Enlightenment as it took form in England, manifesting itself religiously in pietism, and socially in indifferent secularism. Though a group of true English-speaking South Africans began to emerge through time, and though other English-speaking immigrants were seldom overtly British nationalists, there was a general, comfortable reliance on the British Imperial ideal and its governing presence. A unifying mythos of a sort did exist. With the collapse of the Victorian dream and the rapid erosion of British nationalism in South Africa,[7] the anchors in history of English-speaking South Africans became loosened. Meanwhile an opposing force rooted in the country was strongly beginning to emerge - that of Afrikaner nationalism. This grew out ot the sense on the part of Afrikaners (the white group of largely Dutch and some French Huguenot ancestry) of their own oppression at the hand of British imperialism, coupled with their resistance to any change of their already well-established social patterns in accordance with British ideals. White English-speaking South Africans could neither join up with blacks nor ignore the claims of their white Afrikaner fellow-inhabitants, claims stamped on history in the Anglo-Boer War and honoured by Britain in the establishment of the Union of South Africa in 1910 with two Boer i.e. Afrikaner, generals at the country's helm.

It is highly significant that the most neglected group in the formation of Union were the blacks, a factor which gave rise in 1912 to the formation of the largely black African National Congress.[8] English-speaking South

Africans were also significantly neglected insofar as their own role was concerned.

Increasingly shorn of European roots, and later increasingly excluded by Afrikanerdom from effective political participation, English-speaking South Africans were left by and large to play a role from within their liberal democratic heritage (coloured by progressive individualism), or to sink into political apathy while assuring themselves of the 'good life' through economic skills and capital. Any sense of being able to shape history decreased correspondingly, and with it what Ross Snyder refers to as 'the power to understand what is going on'.[9] Thus the loss of an integrative mythos (or 'culture', in the deepest sense) meant the loss of ability to create new meanings.

With this trend came an increasing sense of guilt. This guilt, in the first place, emerged in confrontation with the Afrikaner interpretation of history. Jan Hofmeyer, one of the most prominent men in our history and an English-speaking liberal with Afrikaner roots, indicated the tenor of the Arikaner interpretation in an address to the Eclectic Club of Johannesburg in 1917.[10]

He told them frankly that for the overwhelming majority of Afrikaners, British policy had been one of oppression ... He called the annexation of the diamond fields by Britain in 1871 a robbery, and the annexation of the Transvaal in 1877 a crime. He referred to the fate of the 26,000 Afrikaner women and children who had died in the (British) concentration camps, and advised his hearers to go and contemplate the sombre Vrouemonument at Bloemfontein if they wanted to understand Republicanism.

(He said): It is a painful fact that to the ordinary Dutch-speaking South African the idea of an Englishman naturally arising ... is that of a fearfully superior individual who won't learn his language, who treats him, if not like a piece of dirt, then as being in some grade between his exalted self and his native boy, and who is continually waving over him the glorious folds of the Union Jack.

Such an attitude in English-speaking South Africans is not seldom overtly apparent, yet it remains within the psyche of many.[11] Erik Erikson has pointed to how the historical fate (or at least its memory) of a people becomes for subsequent generations a psychological force.[12] In this sense we may understand English-speaking South African guilt now at the treatment of, and attitude toward Afrikaners in the past, juxtaposed with present lingering prejudices. This, together with the loss of links with the British Empire and its ideal, can now be seen as a psycho-historical force adding to feelings of impotence and defensiveness, and reinforced by the fact that English-speaking South Africans are basically a minority within a minority of whites. Blacks too are now voicing their sense of oppression, and, into the bargain, regard English-speaking South Africans as largely irrelevant to their struggle.

Some try to solve this dilemma by joining in the white, predominantly Afrikaner, Laager[13] - a move that in the short term also bolsters their position as an economic elite. Others attempt to 'help blacks' as much as possible, finding a pseudo-identity in service (more on that point later). Most sink into apathy, happy to live in the narrowed world of contentment offered by economic comfort and social privilege. In most cases, with inordinately few exceptions, there is a lack of paradigms for existence which are positively affirming of self-significance and self-assertion. There is a decisive lack of people and events and institutions which express to a high degree in a particular concrete way the generative expectations of his or her age for the English-speaking South African. There is, in short, a marked lack of archetypal symbols, images, and paradigms which would help us find our way into a new future.[14] To a large extent we now feel ourselves to be the victims of history, caught between the power-blocks of two contesting nationalisms, hoping to find a mediative role here, a supportive roll there, but tremulously uncertain of any role at all. We are patients rather than agents of civilization.[15]

THE FAILURE OF THE LIBERAL DEMOCRATIC TRADITION

Generally English-speaking South Africans may be characterized as secular, individualistic, and pragmatic in the socio-political realm, by and large leaving religious life to take its place within the private personal realm. This is directly related to the milieu of Ninteenth Century British Enlightenment, and the pre-First World War liberal progressive ethos. This tradition is important.

Prevalent in the liberal democratic heritage is an underlying optimism about the goodness of human nature.[16] Thus it still baffles many English-speaking South Africans that an Afrikaner government can so ruthlessly pursue its ideology and so casually rationalize its harshly oppressive laws. Occasional benevolent actions are grasped at as the herald of long-awaited changes, but in vain. And there is a sneaking optimism, totally unwarranted in terms of the actual progression of events, that things will get better, that some kind of absolute Truth and Right will prevail, that Reason will emerge victorious. Finally, there is frequently a naive belief that the economic forces of a so-called 'free-enterprise' system are inherently beneficent.[17]

Based on this tradition we observe the history of English-speaking programs in this century to be largely focused on and around 'educative politics' - the attempt to educate the populace in one way or another to the liberal democratic ideals, using liberal democratic procedures, forms of organization, and institutions, all of which rely on principles of 'fair play', 'allowing the other a voice', and 'maintaining the sanctity of private life'. Anything which operates outside of these bounds becomes perplexing and problematic. Socio-political crises are responded to, but usually by trying to 'heal or cure' the crisis or its effects. Rarely is a radical analysis carried out which will provide a base for an aggressive program to eradicate the preconditions of the crisis insofar as is possible. This illuminates another problem besetting many English-speaking South African socio-political organizations — that most energies and resources are spent on reacting and responding to initiatives taken by others, usually either white Afrikanerdom or black power.

Educative politics shifts into 'reactive politics'; positive proposals, frequently ignored anyway, turn into defensive arguments. The liberal democratic milieu is incapable in many ways of coming to terms with the tenacity of Afrikaner power, its paranoia, and its close-to-absolute determination and willingness to subserve all sectors of society to its own ideals. Furthermore the threat to emerging black power takes its toll. Robert W. Terry of the Detroit Industrial Mission, has said of similar groups in the U.S.A.:[18]

"Helping blacks to bring about racial justice was the benchmark of white participation in civil rights. The vision was lofty and noble ... and should not easily be dismissed. However, inherent in **service** (the liberal ideal) was a fundamental contradiction, namely, that the one serving needed the service."

Moreover, because of the emphasis on treating symptoms or effects, rather than causes,

"Power realities were masked ... Conflict ripped off the mask and found white racism firmly in place, and in motion."

Within all that has been said, lies the inability of English-speaking South Africans to cope adequately with power itself.

PSEUDO-INNOCENCE

Rollo May speaks of authentic innocence as the preservation of a childlike clarity in adulthood, a quality of imagination which does not ignore the reality of evil or one's own complicity with it.[20] In contrast, pseudo-innocence capitalizes on naivete; it shrinks away from reality, refusing to fully recognize real dangers; it wilts before its own complicity in evil and cannot come to terms with destructiveness in itself or in others. It is covert collaboration with evil.

Pseudo-innocence clearly characterizes much of our liberal democratic heritage's bankruptcy. It is precisely in opposition to pseudo-innocence that a leading South African Black theologian, Allan Boesak, has recently published a study on Black Power and Black Theology entitled **Farewell to Innocence.**[21]

Pseudo-innocence is the handmaiden of powerlessness, manifesting itself in either apathy or frenzy - that is, in either attempting to manufacture and secure one's private world on the one hand, or trying fanatically to force reality into one's own mold on the other. In either case there is a failure-of-nerve and a shrinking away from becoming fully human. In either case we become victims of ourselves, and victims of history.[22] In either case there is no generation of spirited existence. We become trapped in our past, lost in our present, and fearful of the future, as we experience a crisis of identity and morale. So it is that Guy Butler, an emminent English-speaking south African, can say of English-speaking South Africans in general:[23]

Behind the facade of our impressive material success, what do we find? A great deal of cynicism and shoulder-shrugging; bitterness and resentment at Afrikaner power; disillusionment at Britain's diminished world stature; fear of, and guilt towards our blacks; and a habit of buck-passing and scape-goat hunting. This lack of confidence is infectious ...

THE ENGLISH-SPEAKING SOUTH AFRICAN CHURCHES

The failure of English-speaking South Africa as a whole is reflected in the failure of the so-called English-speaking South African churches, not so much because of language group affinities as that the churches have allowed themselves to be taken into a Babylonian captivity - of white English-speaking culture. This is perhaps most strongly evident in the orientation of church programs and policies on the basis of liberal democratic procedures. The 'will of the people' who are the membership of the churches, prevails, and it is forgotten that the church is not a democratically organized society at root, but an autocratically organized community with Jesus as Head. This is particularly crucial when it is seen that the hierarchies of the churches are overwhelmingly white dominated to a greater or lesser degree depending on denomination. Thence emerges the frequent inability of the chruches to effectively take up the cause of the poor and oppressed in a situation which cries out for liberation. In fact, as the church historian Peter Hinchcliff points out,[24] the history of the English-speaking South African churches has largely been one of paternalism in relation to blacks, and deference in relation to civil authority. With this goes a sense of being 'the conscience of society'[25] rather than the leaven, an attitude strongly reinforced by liberal ideals. What we have then is a lukewarm Body of Christ, an institution governed all too frequently by the 'lowest-common-denominator' and exhibiting mediocrity in its culture-called the 'breakthrough community'[26], filled with spirited existence.

TOWARDS SPIRITED EXISTENCE

"We wake, if ever we wake at all, to mystery, rumours of death, beauty, violence ..."[27]

The point in trying to understand ourselves and our past, particularly our part in what we frequently blame the Afrikaner government for, is that we should accept our guilt and our complicity in violence as real, and work through it fully. In this way we may realize that we are not simply products of the past, nor need we be bound to the present, in frenzy or in apathy, in powerlessness or in mediocrity.[28] Rather, we may release new energies suspending our present structures of thinking as we risk new formulations and actions in trying to bridge the distance to others.[29]

In doing so, we need first of all to fully appropriate the reality of our relative powerlessness as a minority within a minority. But therein lies not despair - therein lies a blessing in disguise. For we do not have the resources to manipulate the situation; nor shall we ever attempt to compete with Afrikaner or Black nationalism; nor do we have the initiative to nurture Black or Afrikaner power. In those senses we are powerless. But precisely because of that we are free to deal with power at two other levels.

Firstly, we do use exploitative power, and we can begin to find ways of divesting ourselves of that in alternative life-styles and institutions based more on participatory models. Secondly, we can develop integrative power, power that abets the other's power.[30] This is to be "with and for the other",[31] fully accepting the other as they are and being willing to move towards a synthesis of one's own claims and that of the other's. In the South African contest it is clear that this means to accept Black power as essential to our own liberation, and as crucial to blacks[32] in their own struggle for identity and self-affirmation. It also means in a different way to accept Afrikaner power as inevitable, and to confront it with its own paranoia and pretensions to absoluteness. It will not be educated nor persuaded away. And finally it means seeing ourselves not as a power-block, but as a creative minority, refusing any longer to merely respond to the 'will of the people' (especially as that usually means white people). Thus we seek our liberation - from our own racism, from structures of exploitation and privilege, and from our bondage to fear. In short, we seek ways of "expressive living rather than reactive living"[33], of developing programs out of an anticipatory politics rather than an educative politics.[34]

We need to know that the future is going to be very different from the present we cling to. We need to prepare our people for that, and, as the church, we need to know that the victory is already won - liberation is promised. We merely choose, decide how, and endure in the promise - the 'nevertheless'.

It is only as we do this that we as English-speaking South Africans will rediscover the story of our life and the meaning of our journey through history, at the place where the story of our life is inserted into some larger history in a "thrust that includes all other goals.[35]" It is here we may discover the coincidence of a resurgence in our human spirit and the revolution of the Holy Spirit.

In the recovery of morale and the growth of this new identity, we may also discover the meaning of Play, both as the celebration of our promised and partly already experienced freedom with and for others, and, as the laughter that unmasks the pretensions to permanence of the powers and principalities of our time. In authentic innocence, we may face the absurdities of existence without flinching, without renouncing responsibility, and without tolerating the smugness of the powers-that-be.

WAKING FROM THE DEAD

Some ways in which we as a creative minority may move are:

—refusing to play the game of the State on its terms, and thereby developing new strategies of militant non-violent activity. This would be to look into our not-too-distant past, and reclaim, as whites, some of that heritage;

—employing the fact that most of our churches are in principle multi-racial, radically developing that heritage without fear;

— no longer tolerating a pseudo-synthesis based on covert white domination, by ensuring wherever possible that no negotiation, organization, institution, policy-making, or program-planning is any longer based on the manipulations, exploitations, or even ideals of white South Afrca;

— opening up ways of communication where we as whites listen, not for the purpose of doing something about what we have heard (the liberal ideal of service), but to allow decision-making processes to shift to a much greater extent into the hands of blacks;

— being willing, where necessary to deal with our own economic exploitation of others, and the system which allows it;

— imaginatively exploring new alternatives as we look for the significant symbols, the paradigmatic events, the 'rites of passage' which show us the way through the present into a new future;

— organizing for ourselves a new life-space and life-world, where we generate within the present, small and then greater 'liberated zones', areas of life where we with others, both black and white, are already beginning to live as it will be.

In these ways and others we may, "participate in the great creating and redeeming which is going on".[36] We become agents of history, making it more possible for our whole people to arrive at the crucial decision moment when we say "Yes!" to a new future in our history. To quote Ross Snyder again:[37]

'The unforgettable symbol of such moments of decision is the assembling of the tribes of Israel by Joshua. They had escaped from Egypt, but were now wandering in the wilderness. And Joshua said to them: 'Choose this day whom you will serve ... But as for me and my house, we will serve the Lord.' "

By this choice we may once more waken from the dead, and like dry bones in the valley of Ezekiel's vision, we may find ourselves being fleshed with new life in God's liberating work at the Southern end of Africa.

1. Note that the English-speaking churches include those which are predominantly black in membership but whose 'lingua franca' is English, and whose hierarchy is dominated by whites. These include the Methodist Church, the CPSA (Anglican), Presbyterian Church, Baptist Church, Assembly of God (Pentecostal), Congregational Church, Church of England in South Africa.

2. It is important to point out that the term 'white English-speaking S.A.' is sociologically ambiguous. As indicated by L. Schlemmer in 'Identity and Integration', *English Speaking South Africa Today* (ed. A.De Villiers, Oxford Press 1976), an English-speaking S.A'n may be defined as one whose home language orientation is towards English, yet whose ancestry may be otherwise. However most are of British extract.

3. Annie Dillard, *Pilgrim at Tinker Creek*, p. 9 (Bantam Books, 1975).

4. Jung refers to this several times in *Memories, Dreams, and Reflections*.

5. See W. A. De Klerk's treatment of Afrikanerdom in *The Puritans in Africa* (Pelican Books, 1976).

6. I owe this point and the following comment to J.De Gruchy, "English Speaking South Africans and Civil Religion", *Journal of Theology for Southern Africa*, vol. 19, June 1977

7. See Alan Paton, "A Short History of English Nationalism in South Africa", *Pro Veritate*, Jan. 1975

8. The A.N.C. led the black attempt to change white dominated structures, culminating in extensive militant non-violent activity during the first decade or so of Afrikaner rule, only to shift into underground militant opposition on being banned in 1960. An offshoot, the Pan African Congress, was also banned at that time.

9. Ross Snyder, *On Becoming Human* (hereinafter referred to as OBH), Ch. 5 (Abingdon Press, 1967)

10. Alan Paton, *Hofmeyer*, p. 52/3 (Oxford University Press, abridged, 1971). These points are made too, but in relation to blacks, by Archdeacon N.J. Merriman in his journal of 1851 (Dec. 22, in D.H. Varley and H.M. Matthew, eds., *The Cape Journals of Archdeacon N.J. Merriman, 1848-1855*, Cape Town, 1957), and also later by his son, John X. Merriman, a prominent English Speaking South African.

11. A very useful book on the roots of English-speaking South African antipathy toward the Afrikaner is M. Streak's *The Afrikaner as Viewed by the English 1795-1854* (C. Struik Pty, Ltd., Cape Town, 1974).

12. In his psycho-social study of Sioux Indians in particular.

13. A highly defensive closed-circle position of paranoid proportions, adopted when the threat to death seems near - derived from the practice in Voortrekker days of forming ox-wagons into a circle when under attack.

14. It must be said that English-speaking South Africa has generated some prophetic authors who have understood more clearly than most what is happening, and who are trying to reclaim elements of the English-speaking heritage into the building of one South African nation without reference to colour or creed. But their impact has not been sufficient to affect the predominating psyche to any large degree except among some of the more highly educated elite. Some of these authors are Alan Paton, Nadine Gordimer, Athol Fugard.

15. Ross Snyder, OBH, p. 128.

16. See also Harrison M. Wright, *The Burden of the Present*, p. 43 (Rex Collings, London, 1977). This is a very useful and suggestive essay on the liberal-radical controversy over South African history.

17. This has in very recent times become a questionable premise among some, including a few leading capitalists, a development which allows for debate on some important questions.

18. Unpublished paper, "Active New Whiteness: Lighting a Damp Log".

19. This term is borrowed from Rollo May, *Power and Innocence*, (Fontana Paperbacks, 1976). The points made in the following passages rely to a considerable extent on his work.

20. Ross Snyder's notion of authentic human existence is very clearly related to the themes spelled out here. An elaboration of these themes is contained in Snyder's OBH, and in an earlier booklet, *The Authentic Life: Its Theory and Practice* (the 1959 Rufus Jones lecture, revised 1968).

21. Allan Boesak, *Farewell to Innocence*. (Uitgeversmaatschappij J.H. Kok — Kapen, Holland, 1976).

22. Charles Hampden-Turner, *Radical Man*, (Doubleday-Anchor, 1971) refers to this in his psycho-social model, as "Anomie - the failure of existence".

23. F.G. Butler, "The Nature and Purpose of the Conference", *English Speaking South Africa Today*, (op. cit.).

24. In "The English Speaking Churches of South Africa in the Nineteenth Century", *English Speaking South Africa Today*, op. cit. Also published in the *Journal of Theology for Southern Africa*, vol. 9, Dec. 1974.

25. An ecclesiological understanding beginning of course with Constantine.

26. See Dietrich Bonhoeffer, *Life Together*.

27. Annie Dillard, *op. cit.*, p. 2.

28. As Jung says in *Memories, Dreams, and Reflections*, p. 166 (Meridian), "(neurotics) can only regain their health when they climb out of the mud of the commonplace."

29. See Charles Hampden-Turner's model of psycho-social development, op. cit.

30. This delineation of kinds of power is that of Rollo May's, op. cit., p. 105ff. Here he points to Martin Luther King and Mahatma Ghandi as two prime examples in our time, of the use of integrative power.

31. Ross Snyder, OBH, Ch. 6.

32. In the sense in which Rollo May speaks of nutrient power within a people.

33. Ross Snyder, OBH, p. 50ff.

34. Here a clear relationship to theologies of Hope and Liberation is affirmed.

35. Ross Snyder, OBH, p. 19.

36. Ross Snyder, OBH, p. 34.

37. *Ibid.*, p. 39.

Concepts Useful in Comprehending Human Spirit

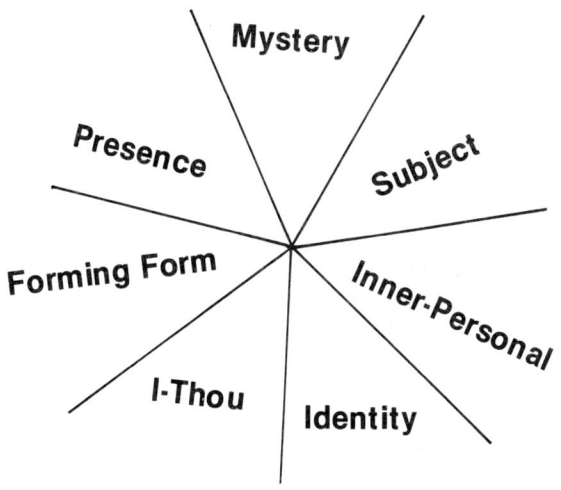

HUMAN SPIRIT

1

A human spirit is a PRESENCE
  It's not a thing. It indwells
    And so has to reveal itself.
A human spirit is a MYSTERY
  A vital center
    with tendrils pervading
      the body and the vitalities of the earth.
  A deep-down exuberance that keeps originating
    Full of darkness, and grace and truth.
An ISNESS
  that principalities and powers did not make or control
Potential
  that is about transcending its present state.
Human spirit is a SUBJECT
  Experiencing itself and the world about it.
    "I experience my self
      I talk with myself
        I think over what happened to me, and work out other options
          I make judgments, I change my mind
            I fight for what I believe in
              I love
                I appeal."
The subject who transmutes lived moments

  into a membrane of language
  and a storied enterprise thru time
   and speaks,
    Expressive spontaneity
     who also hears the human cry
Human Spirit is INNER-PERSONAL
  Where I and ME live
   Where the world is tinctured with I and Me
   Where the internal weather
    enlivens, chokes and pollutes the I and Me
     "I am with
      I am lonely
       Resentful
        Being respected
        Present in my words and action
         I am about to disappear without having fulfilled
         myself.
In the interiority of the Inner-Personal
  Hilaritas prevails ... hibernates ... is depressed
  Inner Speech and conscience and creativity are at home.

2

Spirit becomes an IDENTITY
  A name ... a particularity
   a psychohistory that organizes the inner-personal field
    "I am
     I am **something** ... with some distinctiveness
      I mean it
       I believe in.
  Some people notice me, take account of me
   understand my identity in about the same way I do
    some important events document it.
My Identity is a developing history
  Both continuity and break-out
  An autobiography which combines
  Society's history journey
   The drama of personal center."

3

Human Spirit is I-THOU
  Appreciative consciousness
  An inner population of persons treasured
  A unit of intersubjectivity. Of an ecology of Spirit

4

Spirit is FORMING FORM. Form that **must** develop.
  A helix of generativity
  Putting together
   moments of existence

   symbol clusters
    worlds to live
     inventions of self and sociality
An artesian spring that cannot be contained
 for it is from the depths
Whirlwinds of creation
Lightning-thundering-storming
 in a cosmic game
A helix
 of DNA
A flame
 that develops into destiny
An image of God, intent
 on the ontological
Spirit —
 The only successful
 alchemist
  transmuting earth into meaningfulized world
  producing treasures
   more to be desired than much fine gold
A spectrum of rainbow
 testifying that conversation continues between
  sky and earth
   man and God
    generations
 while mists of promise
 and a slant of light
  Continue to form beauty

5

Spirit —
The bristle-cone pine
  enduring longer than any other tree
  living from roots and leaves if only
   the merest strip of cambium layer still
   functions
    refusing to decay.

* * * *

May you live all your spirit.